CRIME
AND THE
OCCULT

Also by Paul Tabori

Pioneers of the Unseen

CRIME AND THE OCCULT

How ESP and Parapsychology Help Detection

PAUL TABORI

TAPLINGER PUBLISHING CO., INC.
NEW YORK

First published in the United States in 1974 by
TAPLINGER PUBLISHING CO., INC.
New York, New York

Printed in Great Britain

Library of Congress Catalog Card Number: 74-5812
ISBN 0-8008-2028-2

CONTENTS

INTRODUCTION

As a boy in Budapest I grew up inevitably with crime and the occult. My father was an author and journalist, the first modern crime reporter in Hungary, and in the years after World War I, when a wave of occultism swept over the West he also became involved in psychical investigation. Old lags and stool-pigeons regularly visited our apartment, asking for hand-outs and bringing information. One of the books my father wrote was on thieves' slang and he collected the material for it first hand. For several months I regularly startled my teachers by trotting out some shocking expression or picturesque phrase I had picked up from these callers. Father had amassed a vast amount of material, scrupulously filed. He did not, could not know that this would be his death warrant. Many of the leaders of the Arrow Cross Movement, the Magyar version of the Nazis, were common criminals. They took good care to destroy their own records at Police Headquarters but then they discovered that the same information, in even greater detail, was in my father's possession. They arrested him, put him into a cattle truck and shipped him to Auschwitz.

It is a terrible irony that they never found his files which had been removed and kept safe by one of his close friends, the abbot of a Benedictine monastery. In 1946 I was able to recover them and bring them to London.

So it was early enough that I became familiar with burglars, pickpockets, embezzlers, confidence tricksters, forgers and a whole list of law-breakers. Most of them were very well behaved, and though my mother was in constant terror that they would cut our throats or rob us, nothing of this sort ever happened. On the contrary, once Father was warned that a gang of amateurs was planning to burgle our flat; they were arrested even before they could put a jemmy to a window-frame. I found them fascinating though terrible liars, with a peculiar vanity that insisted on a rigid pecking-order, a hierarchy of crime.

With the psychical investigators, the mediums—fake and otherwise—clairvoyants, psychographologists, the specialists in levitation or telekinesis, materialisations or spirit voices, I was less at ease. For one thing many of them were exceedingly comic and a teenager finds it rather difficult to keep a straight face in such encounters. Also, while they were waiting for my father and I had to entertain them, they tried very hard to convert me to whatever theory they had developed, whatever esoteric faith they established as a basis for their activities. I learned about Rosicrucians and the Kabbala, about the Great Pyramid and reincarnation, about auras and ectoplasm—and, inevitably, I felt like the little girl reviewing a long-winded book: 'This tells me more about penguins than I ever wanted to know!'

Sometimes there were more dangerous incidents. One afternoon I had to hide a shivering fake medium in my room while the deaf, high-ranking ex-civil servant whom he had led by the nose for years, had fleeced of his savings and had made thoroughly ridiculous, was crying for his blood.

The sweaty and bug-eyed young man clung to me as if I were his only haven in a storm. Luckily the old gentleman couldn't hear his teeth chattering and, after my father had assured him that the miscreant would be brought to justice, departed. At another time, while Father was away, a huge bearded man called and would not accept my word about his absence. He said he would wait—and it was no use telling him that the person he wished to see would not be back for two days. I hoped that someone, a little older and more authoritative than I, would appear—my mother had no interest in such visitors and kept away from them religiously—when the caller suddenly produced a large kitchen knife and announced at the same time 'I am God.'

There should have been many answers to this startling pronouncement, but the kitchen knife seemed to limit them uncomfortably. It would have been unfortunate had I expressed doubt or disbelief—even if there had been help within screaming distance, my throat could have been cut long before it arrived.

I remembered to bow low—and then I risked this question: 'Which one, oh Lord?'

The huge man swayed a little in the armchair, his immense dark eyes fixed upon me, his fine lips curled in a sneer. 'Don't you know?' he asked with a mild reproach.

'No,' I confessed. 'I mean—you might be Jehovah or Allah. Or even Brahma. Will you enlighten me?'

He didn't. My questions had at least succeeded in confusing him. That was lucky, he might have considered them disrespectful and used the knife to enforce his authority. When he left, after a very uncomfortable half an hour, he turned at the door and said: 'Do not betray me—or I shall never give you the secret of my godhead!'

I pledged my loyalty and then, as soon as he left, went to the bathroom and was sick.

Some years later, though only for a short time, I followed my father's example and became a crime reporter for a big, liberal morning paper. My mentor was a police captain whom I shall call Dr B. He had been a journalist himself and had worked under my father's editorship; he had never forgotten his early, lean years and was kind enough to help me avoid the pitfalls and mistakes few young newsmen could foresee. I dropped in every night at his office and owed him a good many scoops.

One night—it was pretty late, for Dr B practically lived at Police Headquarters—a young man came into the room and asked to be taken into 'protective custody'.

'Why?' asked the captain, 'Are you in danger?'

'Yes,' said the young man, but the danger was himself. He was afraid that he would commit a capital crime and therefore asked to be arrested for twenty-four hours.

Dr B did not laugh nor did he kick him out. He had enough experience with cranks to realise that this young man was out of the ordinary. He offered him a seat (I had withdrawn discreetly to the back of the room), gave him a cigarette and watched him light it with trembling fingers. The young man had long hair, a thin, smoothshaven face and wore tortoise-shell spectacles with tinted lenses. His suit was grey and rather shabby; his thin overcoat's collar was peppered with dandruff, and his tie was askew and carelessly knotted. It was obvious that he was trying very hard to keep his self-control. Dr B tried to reassure him and then asked him to tell his story.

'You'll think me mad,' the young man said. 'And I quite agree, it must be some kind of lunacy that has possessed me. Yet you must take me seriously, my future is at stake—and, what's more important, the lives of two men.'

He spoke fluently enough but now he paused as if finding it difficult to go on.

'I don't know how to make myself clear . . . I'm no criminal. I've never done wrong in my life, I've never had any trouble with the police. And up to this afternoon I was firmly convinced that . . . that I was constitutionally incapable of doing evil . . .'

Again he fell silent, unable to go on. Dr B said a few words of encouragement, trying to draw him out. At last he continued: 'But I was always greatly interested in crime and criminals. That isn't unusual, is it? The papers publish reports, your interest is kindled and you follow the fortunes of the criminal until he is caught; then he is tried and the newspapers are again full of details. Many people follow such trials—perhaps everybody does. I always felt surprised at men who committed a crime deliberately—even murder—in order to obtain a large sum of money—how such men could act so stupidly and blindly, how they could jeopardise their freedom and their life by neglecting some important detail . . Why didn't they work out their plans better? Why didn't they consider every eventuality? Why didn't they guard themselves against discovery and capture? Why did they commit some idiotic act that robbed them of their reward? I spent a lot of time thinking about this. Then I began to plan. What would I do if ever I decided to commit a murder for gain?'

'Well, what *would* you do?' asked the captain. The young man had stopped again. He was trembling.

'Please, do not misunderstand me. I had no intention of committing murder. This was only a . . . a sort of game, a quirk of my imagination. But the game attracted me greatly and I spent much time over it. I realised that in planning such a crime, one mustn't begin with the execution but with the escape.'

'Very good thinking,' smiled Dr B. He made a note on his pad and moved a little closer to his visitor. 'Go on.'

'I had to consider—if I suddenly obtained a large sum, an unusually large amount, a fortune—what would be the next step? How could I make it my acknowledged and unassailable possession without arousing suspicion? I couldn't suddenly appear one day as a rich man—for people knew very well that I wasn't rich. I couldn't go to a bank and deposit my "capital". The bank was bound to ask who I was and where this money had come from. Bankers were much too canny and experienced. Nor could I carry about such a huge sum in my pockets or in a suitcase . . . All this was logical, wasn't it?' He turned to us, for I too had moved closer as he began to overcome his inhibitions and warm to his tale.

Dr B nodded.

'Well, Captain,' the young man continued, 'first I had to settle the bank business, with proper foresight and care. The place where I was to deposit the money had to know me and consider me absolutely trustworthy. They had to know in advance that I was going to deposit such and such a sum on a particular day and had to be prepared for my instructions to transfer the money abroad. The foreign bank, too, had to be informed in advance and instructed that, once the transfer had taken place, the money was to be paid against a particular signature of the rightful owner who would call on a definite date. Of course I had no intention of paying the whole sum into one bank nor of splitting it into equal parts. Therefore, a year or so before I was to commit the crime, I had to open accounts in several banks.'

The captain raised his hand.

'Did you? Do you actually have such accounts?'

'Yes, I did—and I have them. One is with a private bank. I know its president. The others are at the local branches of various big banks in different districts—in each case I know the manager. I have saved about 2,000 pengős for capital . . .' (At that time a pound was roughly worth twenty-five pengős.) 'I manipulated this sum, withdrawing, paying in, giving small commissions to buy foreign currency and sell it again. About once every four weeks I visited the different banks to discuss my financial affairs, listened to the managers' advice, chatted about my plans and prospects. They all knew me as a small but completely reliable client.'

'Are your accounts under assumed names?'

'No, why should they be? I didn't want to complicate things needlessly . . . Please, Captain, remember there's no serious purpose behind all this. It's just a game, an experiment—nothing more.'

'I understand.'

'Now, one needs at least 2 million pengős to live abroad without having to work and the big industrial firms need cash at the end of each week to cover the payrolls. This is fetched from the banks by special messengers, as you know. If you pick a day upon which both weekly and monthly wages and salaries have to be paid, a total of 2 or 3 million pengős is not unusual. They usually pick two messengers for such an important job; happily, we have no armoured cars or police guards in this country as there have been no American-style payroll robberies here. Robbery would offer little prospect of success in the bank, on the street or in the factory offices. It is necessary therefore to lure the messengers to one's home. For this it is essential to be on intimate terms with them. But you must not be so friendly that the police, looking for their friends or acquaintances, are able to trace you. All this I discovered by pure deduction. Do you agree, Captain?'

'I think your deductions are extremely shrewd. Did you try to put them into practice?'

'Yes, I sought such friendships. Why not, Captain? It is not illegal and it gave me pleasure to spin a net. Eventually, however, I decided to give up . . .'

'I believe you—yet you came here tonight . . .'

'It became my custom to sit in the waiting rooms of the big banks. On certain days the messengers also sit there, waiting to be called. I joined them—pretending to wait as they did . . .'

'Have you nothing else to do?'

'Of course I have. I work for an important business firm, for which I travel constantly as a representative, and no one can check on my movements. The question was, how to approach the bank messengers? They were all hand-picked, middle-aged, reserved and dutiful, and of course they were also cautious and suspicious men. It was difficult to gain their confidence. I thought the best way would be to find out their hobbies and exploit their passions. They all must have some hobby, I reasoned, and I was right. One of them was a devoted philatelist, the other a great lover of music, the third had become deeply interested in Marxism and its literature. Yet all this was somehow not enough. There had to be something else—some deep urge . . . One morning I sat down in the waiting room with a saucy magazine in my hand. Several of the messengers stopped and glanced at the pages over my shoulder, then two of them sat down beside me, borrowed the paper and studied it together. That was the beginning. The next day I showed them some erotic pictures—the usual kind. They got very excited and so I told them I had plenty more at home, even better ones, and I suggested they dropped in one day. And they did—unsuspecting and happy.'

Dr B slammed down his hand on his desk-top. 'Amazing! And very clever. But still quite legal . . .'

'At first they called on me when off-duty; they looked at my erotic books, my drawings, my photographs; they could not see enough of them. You must understand, I had no interest in all this—I only collected the stuff for them. It's easy enough to get these things if you're willing to spend time and money. Now they often visit me even when they're on duty without a second thought, just for ten minutes to admire my latest "acquisitions". On such occasions they carry the money with them. They are solid, married men—a little henpecked, maybe. They are under constant supervision, they daren't make any slip, they don't even long for any escapades. But there is a certain unfulfilled longing for adventure, however vicarious, in all of them. So they satisfy it through their imaginations. Their conscience remains clear. Of course, they're a bit careless, bringing their sealed and locked bags with them, but they know me—and there are, after all, always two of them. Safety in numbers, you know.'

He lit a cigarette, then resumed his unemotional account.

'Do I look like a criminal, Captain? Believe me, I'm not. It's just that playing with fire attracts me, but I know it can never become serious. This week the pay-day for weekly wages and monthly salaries falls on the same day, and tomorrow my two particular friends are going to collect the money from the bank—at least a million and a half. I only have to tell them that some "new stuff" has arrived. That's our password—and they'll come rushing to my apartment as they have done twenty times before.'

'Where do you live?' I asked, speaking for the first time.

'I have rented an apartment from someone else—a long way from my own furnished room. The bank messengers, however, think it's my only home—while the landlord believes I merely use it to work and receive customers. I paid the rent in advance; they don't even know my name. Should the police call, no one could give them any information. My landlady won't miss me. At the office I have asked for a few weeks off. When I'm already on my way, I intend to inform my employers that I've found a better job. They won't enquire about me. I've neglected my appearance a little but this rather shabby figure is only a persona I've gradually built up over the last two years. In my apartment I have a well-pressed new suit, a spotless set of linen. After I have done what I have to do, I'll cut my hair, take off these glasses. (At the various banks I'm known without spectacles, anyhow.) My suitcases are at the station, my passport is in order, I have all my tickets on me. I have picked the train—I even know which carriage I'm to travel in. Before anyone can discover that the bank messengers are missing, I'll be on my way, and by the time the crime has become public knowledge, I'll be safely across the frontier. No shadow of suspicion can touch me. And once abroad, I can take a week to collect my capital; everything will be in order, according to my instructions, on the basis of my authorised signature. Within a year I'll be in undisputed possession of my loot.'

'Wait a minute,' interrupted the captain. 'For the time being that money is still with the bank messengers and not in your hands?'

'Of course. When my regular guests sit down at my table and have become absorbed in enjoying my new pictures, I intend to place three glasses in front of us. I shall produce a bottle of brandy, fill the three glasses and replace the bottle in the cupboard. Then I toast them; they empty their glasses while I only drink half my share. A little later I bring out the bottle again and fill up—but only their glasses. Once again we drink—they have their second glass, I finish my first. This is how it happens every time and it will be the same tomorrow. I've conditioned them for it.'

'And then?'

'There is a second bottle in my cupboard. It contains brandy—with a little something added. Prussic acid. If I so wish, their second glassful is poured out of this bottle.

And as soon as they've drunk it, they're practically dead . . .'

'Well, I'll be . . .' Dr B rose.

'Of course, I don't intend to do all this,' repeated the young man, 'Why should I? I have merely designed the whole scheme for my own entertainment—just to prove to myself how sanely and safely I can plan. I can just as well pour the drinks from the first brandy bottle the second time; they finish their drink, spend another ten minutes with me, go on their way and the game is over. I pledged myself that it shall be so.'

'And you will keep your pledge,' smiled the captain. 'You are an honest and intelligent man. It would be even better if you did not go to the bank tomorrow and did not invite the messengers any more to your place. It would be best if you put an end to this game of planning and plotting and never met them again . . .'

'You're certainly right, Captain. Quite right. But there's something . . .' The young man glanced at the door as if weighing the chances of escape. 'Something I haven't foreseen. Now that the machinery is all prepared, it may start to function . . . automatically. I planned a crime carefully—because I thought I would be unable to commit it. Now it has become so easy. It almost looks . . . necessary and unavoidable. Suddenly I am afraid—afraid of myself . . .'

'But if you don't *want* to do it . . . why should you?'

'I can't explain, why. Please, Captain, lock me up. Only for a day. By tomorrow evening—no, tomorrow noon —I will have lost my opportunity. The payrolls will have been delivered, my ticket expired, and I will have missed the dates of paying in the various amounts and transferring them. I won't go through all this rigmarole a second time. Everything depends on a single hour, tomorrow morning . . . Please, save me . . . help me!'

He was trembling again. Dr B started to pace the room.

'Look,' he said, swinging round, 'this is not so easy. I can't arrest you without a good reason—I'd be guilty of a wrongful arrest. You must have committed a crime first and, according to your own story, you haven't done anything illegal. Where did you get the prussic acid from?'

'I distilled it myself—from almonds.'

'There you are . . . No law forbids that. You've acted too cleverly. Why should I arrest you?'

'For protection.'

'From what? Are you drunk and disorderly? Are you mad? Is some gang menacing you? Just because you talk of plans and ideas . . . taking steps anyone is perfectly entitled to take? I'm a policeman and a guardian of the law. I cannot arrest you—until you have committed a crime . . .'

'By then it will be too late.'

There followed a long, fruitless argument. Then Dr B turned to me. For some reason that I couldn't explain, I suddenly became highly irritated with the young man.

'I think this is just a silly farce,' I sneered, 'I don't believe a word of your story. Maybe you're destitute and just want to spend a few comfortable days in jail. But prisons aren't like hostels . . .'

He protested hotly. He had his home, he had a job.

'Have you?' I pressed him. 'Well, prove it. Show us your papers, your ticket . . .'

'I can't do that.' Again, he glanced at the door. 'I wish you wouldn't insist . . . because, after all, if I should . . .'

Dr B intervened.

'Well then, go home—and go to bed. If you don't *want* to commit a crime, there's no possible need for you to do so. But if you carry it through, we'll find you, don't worry . . .'

The young man took his hat and coat reluctantly. The captain stepped to him and put his hand on his shoulder.

'I don't share my young friend's views,' he said, glancing

at me, 'I don't think your story incredible, but I can't help you. I must stick to the rules. Take hold of yourself. Don't yield to temptation. Think of the grave penalties involved . . . think of the wrong you would commit . . . the two honest men you'd kill . . . their innocent families you'd deprive of all support. Think of your own parents. If you don't *want* to, you won't do it . . .'

'No, no, of course not. If I don't want to, I . . .'

He dragged himself out of the room, closing the door quietly.

I looked at Dr B. Our eyes met. He shrugged and sat down at his desk. We were both silent for a long time. Then my mood changed again and I was sorry for the young man. It was too late to follow him and . . .

'You really couldn't have accommodated him?' I asked the captain.

He shrugged.

'Maybe I could've stretched the point. But I didn't *really* believe his story. You know how many people we get confessing to a crime during an investigation who had nothing to do with it? Exhibitionists, cranks . . . a legion. The only difference here was that he confessed to a crime before the fact.' He added, after a little pause: 'Besides, the bell didn't ring.'

I wanted to ask him what he meant by this but at that moment the bell *did* ring—the phone shrilled. A hold-up in a jeweller's shop. The criminals had escaped and had killed a policeman who was trying to stop them. In the exciting hours that followed we both forgot the disturbed strange young man and his elaborate plot.

I didn't finish writing my story until the small hours and then went home to catch up on my sleep. In any case, it was my day off and I had planned to take my girl-friend on a Danube outing. It wasn't until late in the evening that I got back to my apartment. I found three messages from Dr B, asking me to get in touch with him immediately. I phoned and he told me to come round to his office. I asked him what had happened but he refused to give me any details, and his voice sounded strange, a little hoarse and hesitant, very unlike his usual self.

I arrived at Police Headquarters just after midnight. The usually dapper captain sat in shirtsleeves, his collar open, his hair tousled; the ashtray on his desk was overflowing.

'He's done it,' he greeted me and I did not have to ask to whom he was referring. 'The two bank messengers were found late this afternoon—both dead. Prussic acid. The bank isn't certain but they think some 2 million pengős are missing.'

'And the young man . . .?'

'We still don't know his real name nor anything else about him. It was only by an accident that his landlord entered the apartment he had rented under a false name—there was a burst pipe on the floor above and they wanted to check whether any flooding had occurred . . . By now, of course, he must have crossed the frontier. And we don't know *which* frontier—north, south, west, east . . .'

He added, in a low voice, almost to himself: 'That's bad enough—but there's even worse . . .'

He turned to me again: 'I must ask you a great favour—and I shall understand if you refuse. Nor can I presume upon my friendship with your father . . .'

'My dear Dr B—I owe you so much. Anything I can do . . .'

'It's something I want you *not* to do. You have a scoop in your hands, a journalist's dream. You were here when this man told his story. I want you to forget about it—completely.

I swallowed hard but naturally I had no choice.

'Yes, of course.'

'Maybe, one day, you can. Secrets have short lives. If we catch him, he might very well use it in his own defence, but until then . . .'

'I told you,' I reassured him, for he seemed to be in need of reassurance, 'But I have one question to ask—what did you mean when you said "the bell didn't ring"?'

He lit another cigarette. He appeared to be a little calmer; he even smiled.

'I'll answer your question—but that's another off-the-record statement. Statistics are the devil's snare, but out of a hundred crimes, world-wide, actually committed, at least fifteen are never reported—out of fear, stupidity or laziness. Of the remaining 85 per cent, if you take the global average, half are never solved.'

'That's a pretty poor record—and I'm sure quite a few police officials would deny it.'

'Officially, yes; privately, no. So let us stick to the forty-odd cases out of every hundred. My own average, by the way and as you know yourself, has been nearer 70 or 80 per cent. I'm not bragging about it—but why do you think I have been about twice as successful as most of my colleagues?'

'Surely you are not fishing for compliments? You are a very good policeman. You use the most modern methods in ballistics, dactyloscopy, forensic chemistry . . .'

'Poppycock.'

I stared at him, now completely puzzled.

'There is no proper word to describe it,' he continued, noticing my reaction, 'Intuition is much too weak, inspiration is much too presumptuous. I call it the "bell ringing". Clues are all very well; confessions are even better. But there is a sixth sense which some of us possess—or develop, like a wine-taster's palate or a perfume-maker's nose. It has worked for me a thousand times—so I have come to rely on it whenever I meet some problem that isn't just an open-and-shut case. It is some force that bridges the gap between the known and the unknown, that tells me, almost unerringly, whether a man speaks the truth or not, where I have to go to pick up a weapon, a piece of clothing, a spent bullet; it makes the murkiest motivations clear and opens the locked doors . . .'

He stopped suddenly as if ashamed of his own eloquence. He shook his head.

'It has never failed before. Do you understand why I am worried? Do you agree that this is not something that can be published?'

'I do, I do. But everybody is entitled to fail, to make a mistake once in a while. I certainly wouldn't worry about it . . .'

But even as I spoke, I realised that he was barely listening to me.

Three months later Dr B committed suicide. He left no note and the official statement spoke of 'constant overwork . . . great strain . . . a brilliant career'. The young man who had planned his crime with such diabolic skill and who had lost the battle with his moral inhibitions (though he gained a cool two million) was never found although his identity was finally established.

This is a book about the late Dr B's 'ringing bell', about crime and the occult. It does not deal with fake mediums, phoney astrologers, fraudulent fortune-tellers, false prophets and the countless exploiters of human credulity and stupidity: they could easily fill another half-a-dozen volumes. Instead, it is devoted to criminal investigation and detection, using the methods that are inexplicable in terms of orthodox and materialistic science.

It is, of course, necessary to define our terms of reference. There are a great many semantic interpretations of the word *occult*. The more popular include: 'supernatural, mystical, magical'. The one truly pertinent to our own subject is less esoteric: 'Kept secret; recondite, mysterious, beyond the range of ordinary knowledge'. And this is perhaps more acceptable to those who would shudder at the idea that a policeman should be using his ESP powers instead of his notebook; that clairvoyance could produce faster and more reliable results than a microscope. It would be, of course, equally stupid to claim that in a good many cases 'normal' police procedures do not achieve their goal. But one does not exclude the other. Many experts have sounded the warning that if the urban sprawl continues, if our ecological lunacy is given free hand, we will drown in our own filth. Equally strong warnings have been voiced about the problem of crime. We can still punish but we can rarely prevent—as Dr B could have prevented the young man's crime if his 'bells' had been ringing. More than half of the police's time is spent on ridiculous trivia –collecting drunks, towing away cars, checking licences. They are certainly not in the position to refuse help from any quarter if it is forthcoming.

But is it? Would anybody advocate that the police department of every big city should recruit a staff of telepaths, psychics and sensitives? That crystal balls and ouija boards should become regulation equipment in every station and precinct?

Hardly.

The main difficulty of the acceptance of occult phenomena has always been that they rarely, if ever, can be produced on command. Scientists are irritated and discouraged by the fact that they cannot apply the methods of research to materialisations or telekinesis. Whatever happens, obeys its own laws which have *not* been established; which may not even exist. And, of course, a good deal of it is sheer fakery. What would be the use of employing mediums in police work if they could not guarantee to function as rationally and regularly as infra-red photography or chemical analysis? Who would depend on 'flashes of insight', 'telepathic communications', 'supernatural inspiration' as long as there were files, machines and just good old-fashioned legwork?

However, it is a fact that the police of many countries *have* relied on such disreputable folk, accepting that they could not always or even frequently present the required results. They just count their blessings, although, of course, in quite a few places they still fight shy of the psychic.

Another fact is that, without disparaging forensic science, not even its most prominent representatives would claim infallibility for its results. Only recently a dactyloscopic expert came clean and confessed that it was practically impossible to obtain usable prints from a gun. Poisons have been discovered that leave absolutely no traces (a godsend to detective story writers); but at the same time natural, non-poisonous substances have been found that could cause death under certain circumstances and indicate the presence of toxins. The whole field of biochemistry has opened up immense possibilities for apprehending the criminal—and for mistakes. Every war, as we know, brings a vast technological upsurge although we always have to pose the question as to whether this could not have been achieved without the hecatombs of millions. We are only at the beginning of the revolution which the side-products of space travel, of computer technology or of miniaturisation have wrought. What it all means for the police is simple enough: the need for increasingly greater sophistication, and the rising danger of being left behind in the race between machine and man, the use and abuse of power. There is less and less certainty in this age of nuclear physics and cosmology; it is now possible to demonstrate Einstein's relativity theory, quite convincingly, to the illiterate and the virtual moron. There is more and more need for an open mind, for experimentation, for the acceptance of entirely new concepts and possibilities—even in such a pragmatic profession as that of a policeman.

But hasn't imaginative, creative detection *always* used these possibilities?

Here is the great ancestor of them all, Monsieur C. Auguste Dupin, bearing witness: 'They [the police] have no variation of principle in their investigations; at best, when urged by some unusual emergency, by some extraordinary reward, they extend or exaggerate their old modes of *practice,* without touching their principles . . .'

And though a fanatic of logic, of pragmatic practicability himself, he adds: 'The material world abounds with very strict analogies to the immaterial . . .'

We know that the purloined letter was found by this intuitive reasoning—far more intuitive than Poe would himself admit—in defiance of the orthodox forensic methods.

There have been psychoanalytic interpreters of the great American master's work who actually argued that he invented Dupin as a counter-balance to the world of intangible menace that was closing in upon him, a world which he exploited so richly and brilliantly in his tales of horror and imagination.

What of the great sage of 222b Baker Street? We know that he was a morphine addict—though he was obviously able to control the habit and its effects did not impair his talent. Sir Arthur does not tell us whether Sherlock Holmes sought the kind of psychedelic, 'mind-enlarging' experience in morphine that Dr Leary's disciples are seeking today in LSD. But Holmes's methods confuted again and again the orthodox police investigator—like Dupin, he had the representatives of the law panting behind, clumsy and unseeing—while he reconstructed, as today's identikit pictures do, a whole personality from a few strands of tobacco, a footprint, a smear of paint, duly astonishing the faithful Dr Watson who existed for the purpose of being astonished.

There is almost nothing in the Holmes stories that forecast the conversion of Sir Arthur to spiritualism in his later years. But Sherlock Holmes, perhaps prophetically, has certain qualities of a medium—a psychometrist. His reaction to objects, ordinary and normally insignificant, is very often that of a psychic 'giving a reading' while he or she is holding some personal possession and deriving from it (or claiming to do) images and conclusions supernaturally. The great fictional detective and his creator would of course have denied such a resemblance, but if you go through the Holmes stories carefully, you will find it confirmed again and again.

With Chesterton's Father Brown we are in the world of total intuition based on the strong pillars of ethics and religion. 'The mind of the little priest was always a rabbit-warren of wild thoughts that jumped too quickly for him to catch,' his creator wrote characteristically. He, too, uses facts to bring miscreants to justice—but he uses them, in obedience to Chesterton's love of paradox, by standing them on their heads. This new perspective enables him to deduce the truth; the mysterious, the unfamiliar, the contradictory are accepted as part of reality and help to restore the balance disturbed in the world of morality, of Christian faith. To Chesterton, the Catholic convert, all crime was a crime against God, and human justice was secondary to the restitution of the divine order, the penitence of the sinner and his redemption. Father Brown has been described as a 'practical mystic', a sort of twentieth-century postulant (in all modesty) to the status of St Francis of Assissi.

Elements of the occult, in the sense we have defined it, can be easily traced in scores of other fictional detectives and I hope one day someone does a whole book on this aspect alone. The elements are present however much the authors might deny it or be unaware of it—in the little grey cells of Monsieur Poirot, in the silly-ass camouflage of Lord Peter Wimsey, in the short-lived career of Philip Trent—to mention only a few of the most celebrated. But of course these examples are easy to dismiss for, after all, they are only the fancies of story-tellers. (This, however, does not quite fit in with the recurrent accusations that crime writers, by describing ingenious methods of murder, forgery and fraud, encourage emulation. It may be true that life often emulates art, but even if you learn from some thriller how to prepare a poisonous potion or blow a safe, no 'do-it-yourself' kits are provided.) I have mentioned Poe and his successors because they sum up and embody in their great fictional detectives the experience of hundreds of real-life policemen; the true artists among them combine sound research with the talent of presenting action, character and motive clearer and more convincingly than confused and contradictory newspaper reports or documentary accounts.

However, there is ample evidence that the occult element in criminal investigation has been recognised and even advocated in actual practice.

More than fifty years ago, Professor Antal Hermann, a distinguished sociologist, argued for wider acceptance of 'the science of metaphysics and of suggestive powers', and their use on a scientific basis in modern criminology. They should be employed, he said, not only by the police forces but also in prisons. The professor was official consultant to the

Hungarian Home Office at that time and he voiced truly revolutionary ideas for those early years.

'I have discussed these matters,' he told me, 'with leading officials of the Home Office, the police and the *gendarmerie* and they have no objection to such experiments. After all, many of our active detectives work with what one might call their sixth senses. Just as the science of graphology has already been recruited for police work—though this, too, was for a long time considered mere superstition—we must not despise the powers of suggestion. We have quite a lot of people with hypnotic powers who are, however, insufficiently trained. Experiments which in the beginning are inevitable failures must not discourage us, for in other countries modern criminology has used the occult sciences in many places with considerable success. Nor must we be frightened by the words "occult sciences" just because a whole host of tricksters and demagogues have abused them. Some of the powers that in recent years wanted to overthrow the long-established, traditional order with their underground organisations were, in their psychological structure, occult in a certain sense—so our defence must also rest on occult premises. Metaphysics is a powerful, comprehensive field, embracing the outlines of a new world—so criminal investigation cannot ignore it.'

These were quite extraordinarily committed statements by a conservative and cautious educator and high-ranking civil servant; I do not think that they would be echoed today with such explicit firmness. Yet Professor Hermann summed up, in a way, the whole subject of this book. If the resistance of scientists and police officials alike has lessened in certain respects—no one would gainsay the employment of handwriting experts today while fifty years ago they still had to fight for recognition—in other respects it has hardened, become a good deal more widespread. The consultation of clairvoyants and mediums usually takes place in the less orthodox police departments and even there only as an *ultima ratio*, when there is nothing else left.

I attended in the early thirties a meeting of the Viennese Criminological Association (Kriminalistische Vereinigung) devoted entirely to the discussion of the employment or utilisation of the 'so-called occult phenomena' in police procedure and judicial investigation. A large number of physicians and lawyers were present; the best-known specialists in criminal cases rubbed shoulders with neurologists, forensic psychiatrists and medical specialists. The chair was taken by Dr Altmann, President of the Viennese *Landesgericht* or High Court. His opinion was that telepathy could have its disadvantages because it might mislead rather than help the investigator. But Dr Siegfried Türkel, a very well-known criminal lawyer, the first speaker, described in great detail the importance of research into telepathy, clairvoyance and hypnosis. According to him telepathy was based on muscular hyperaesthesia and a deductive talent for combining widely varied elements; in his view only clairvoyance could be important for criminology. Dr Kogerer, attached to the Psychiatric Clinic, argued that for the physician there could be no occult sciences; hypnosis was a phenomenon which had been thoroughly studied by medicine but that it would be of little use to police investigation as it was, in his view, impossible to make a criminal confess under hypnosis. However, it might be possible that under the influence of hypnosis a person who for some reason wished to shield the criminal, could be persuaded to drop this attitude and so provide useful evidence. In contrast to hypnosis, Dr Kogerer said, telepathy has not yet become truly accessible to scientific study as the experiments conducted up to now were undertaken under unsatisfactory conditions; the lack of exact observations excluded at present the utility of telepathy and clairvoyance.

Dr Paul Schilder, another assistant professor, also emphasised that all his experiments with the well-known clairvoyant Hanussen and with a doctor who was alleged to have telepathic talents have turned out to be negative. Telepathy seems to function—if it *does* function—in a purely arbitrary, irregular manner even when, as some researchers claim, it can be proved to occur. So it can be hardly recommended for forensic purposes. He, too, excluded hypnosis from use in police work. He had treated a woman at the psychiatric clinic who had tried to commit suicide by an overdose of sleeping pills. She had obtained these pills from a nurse; but not even in deep-layer hypnosis would she disclose the nurse's name. As hypnosis depended to a considerable extent on a sympathetic connection being established between hypnotist and subject, it was possible that in some cases confessions could be obtained by it, but it was highly questionable whether in criminal investigation such 'erotic influences' could be justified for such an end. It was a different matter when witnesses were questioned. In deep hypnosis someone might be reminded of details which he could not produce in a waking state.

There were more positive voices at the meeting. Dr Thoma, a police superintendent, worked regularly with a clairvoyant medium and had only a few days earlier solved a particularly complex case with her help. He and an attorney named Dr Richard Pressburger argued that *practice* proved the value of the occult in police investigations and that it was equally foolish to reject it because of initial failures or deny its usefulness because of the lack of a coherent theory to explain its workings.

In 1973 I went to Paris to talk to a high-ranking French police official who insisted on anonymity. The gist of our long talk was an enthusiastic endorsement of the occult, in the widest sense of the word, as a means of combating and solving crimes. His motivation was particularly interesting.

'Criminals,' he said, 'are the most superstitious folk in the world. One could compile an encyclopaedia about the various taboos, shibboleths and crazy beliefs of burglars and hold-up men, forgers or smugglers. It is only natural that we should utilise this circumstance to foil them and catch them. I have no hesitation in using mediums, clairvoyants, fortune-tellers or astrologers in my work. Their record is far from 100 per cent successful; but then, they compare quite favourably with the orthodox, plodding police work—in spite of computers, Interpol, satellite communications and all the rest. The machine, the advanced technology often cannot deal with the individual—and each criminal is very much a unique personality however hackneyed his methods, repetitious his tricks.'

In this short volume we are going to deal with the various areas of parapsychology, of extra-sensory functions within the context of criminology—with hypnosis, psychographology, the various mediums engaged regularly or occasionally in police work, with dowsing and allied practices, with witchcraft and finally with the occult elements in forensic medicine and penology. Inevitably, the part will have to serve for the whole—each of these chapters could be easily expanded into a whole independent book—nor is it possible to tell each story with a proper beginning, middle and end. Testimony must be reported without embellishment, but the conclusions drawn must be the reader's.

I would like to offer special thanks to Mr Stan Farnsworth of Halifax, Nova Scotia, for his enthusiastic and valuable help.

P.T.

1

SVENGALI'S HEIRS

In November 1920 Professor Julius von Wagner-Jauregg, the famous neurologist and psychiatrist (and future Nobel Prize laureate for physiology and medicine), was sitting in his study in Vienna when his manservant announced a visitor. It was a well-dressed woman, wearing a fur-coat and carrying a muff. She greeted the professor pleasantly enough, handed him a letter and, as he began to open it, she drew a gun from her muff, pointed it at Wagner-Jauregg—and then, just as suddenly, dropped it. Whether she had pressed the trigger or not, could not be ascertained—but certainly, the gun did not go off.

The great alienist made her sit down; she was trembling violently and behaved in a wild, confused manner. The police were called and she was taken away. The police surgeon who examined her diagnosed 'advanced hysterics' and she was sent for further examination and treatment to Wagner-Jauregg's own clinic.

There some of the professor's assistants began to probe her mind. She told them that her name was Maria D and that an engraver named G had hypnotised her several times. She could not remember anything that had happened in Wagner-Jauregg's consulting room. One of the psychiatrists proceeded to hypnotise her—she proved to be an excellent subject—and commanded her to tell all she knew. She readily obeyed this command and related how, two days before her 'attempt at murder', G hypnotised her, put a blank cartridge into a gun and ordered her to fire it. Then he reloaded the gun and told her to call on Professor Wagner-Jauregg with the letter he handed her and fire a shot at him. Maria D asked several questions but G assured her that the whole thing was an experiment, that the professor would come to no harm nor was there any danger to herself and it would be excellent publicity which might lead to a music hall engagement.

It was only gradually that the motive of the strange affair was uncovered—and even then there was a measure of contradiction. It could not be hostility to the distinguished alienist for he was no opponent of hypnosis; his own clinic used it. The Viennese papers created a great hullabaloo about the incident—but it had nothing to do with any argument about the validity or the dangers of hypnotism. Rather, there was one particular point at stake. Wagner-Jauregg had stated repeatedly that it was impossible to turn anybody into a criminal by hypnotic suggestion. Now, some of the papers hinted maliciously, the engraver G had succeeded in proving him wrong. Even politics entered into it—the left-wing *Arbeiterzeitung* saw in the rather trivial event the struggle of the 'capitalist' Wagner-Jauregg and the 'proletarian' G, a conflict between the Establishment and a free, bold spirit.

But, of course, Wagner-Jauregg was right. In his book, published in 1919 under the title of *Suggestion, Hypnotism and Telepathy*, he wrote: 'Because of the great influence which the hypnotist acquires over his medium, it must be admitted as an *a priori* possibility that someone receives the suggestion of a criminal act which he carries out during the trance or in case of post-hypnotic suggestion, at a later date . . . But in spite of the fact that the argument has raged for forty years, no absolutely trustworthy and documented case of such suggestion has been recorded.'

Actually, the argument still seems to rage. In his *Kompendium der medizinischen Hypnose* (Compendium of Medical Hypnosis), an introduction into medical practice, Professor D. Langen, director of the University Clinic and Polyclinic for Psychotherapy in Mainz, is quite unequivocal about it: 'Again and again we encounter the statements that criminal acts can be committed under hypnosis. But such statements are practically never tenable. (Hammerschlag collected some rather curious cases in 1954.)'

Hypnotism has been defined as the artificially induced state of heightened suggestibility. Suggestion can only consist of what the medium *wishes* to be suggested, something his imagination can embrace; just as even our most fantastic dreams are made up of already existing, known elements. 'An action as a human attitude determining will and decision,' Professor Langen elaborated, 'in the sense of doing or not doing something can only be effected by hypnosis or suggestion if it corresponds to the normative strivings of the personality involved.' Krafft-Ebing was even more crushing: 'Hypnotic crime,' he said, 'only exists in the imagination of novelists who rely on laboratory experiments and not the experiments of real life.'

Such laboratory experiments were said to prove that even under hypnosis the subject did not surrender his or her will power completely and that even highly sensitive people only accepted suggestions which were 'in harmony with their mental make-up'. The experiments in which the hypnotic command was to kill someone did not provide proof, the experts said. The medium who had taken part in such experiments before knew only too well that for the sake of proving a scientific point the hypnotist won't take a life—that the whole thing was only play-acting, a staged comedy.

In the case of Wagner-Jauregg, too, G assured Maria D repeatedly that firing the gun could not cause the professor harm, and the girl even stepped back so that the wad of paper should not burn her 'victim'. G also promised her considerable financial advantages if she carried out his command; this might have actually roused the desire in her to try the experiment. In fact, Maria D could only be persuaded under hypnosis to do what she herself wished to do.

There have been similar cases. One of Wagner-Jauregg's assistants tried in vain to persuade a woman whom he had hypnotised to undress in the presence of others. But whenever she was alone with him, she started to take off her clothes without the slightest hesitation—for she only saw the doctor in him. Professor Delboeuf reported the case of a woman who lived in the same house with him. She kept a loaded revolver under her pillow, and on one occasion she had, by her brave defiance, sent some burglars running for their lives.

Delboeuf decided to try an experiment with her. He called her into his room, put her into a hypnotic trance as soon as she entered (he had hypnotised her before); then he pointed to the two men who were rummaging in his desk. 'These are burglars,' he said, 'they want to rob me of my bonds!' Thereupon the lady walked up to them and called on them firmly to leave the professor's property alone. At Delboeuf's command she hurriedly fetched her revolver, but though he called on her several times to fire (he had removed the bullets) she refused to do so—for she had every reason to believe the gun to be loaded.

To the layman the belief that you could force someone by hypnosis to commit a crime seemed harmless enough. But the psychiatrists did not think so. If the idea spread, criminals would put up the defence that they had acted under hypnosis with increasing frequency; or they might even get themselves hypnotised so that they should have an alibi. In central Europe, at least, there have been parallel cases when someone asked his companions to get him drunk, so that he could commit a crime and claim diminished responsibility. And while it was agreed that it was possible to suggest the commission of crimes by hypnotic and post-hypnotic command, up to the 1920s there had been no authentic recorded case in medical literature in which an individual of normal mental and moral qualities committed any crime under hypnotic suggestion, or in which the complete subjection to the hypnotist's will was the only motive of the crime. The experiment staged by G was only a 'laboratory crime' because the method of the test was unsuitable and the medium herself knew that she was only play-acting.

Dr Thoma and Megalis

The Wagner-Jauregg episode led to a widespread discussion among forensic experts as to whether hypnotism could be used in criminal invesigation. Would it be possible to induce clairvoyance in a hypnotic state, enable a suitable medium to describe the details of a crime and the criminal?

It was then that Dr Leopold Thoma, the retired superintendent of police who had become an attorney, presented some of his cases; he had been unable to do so earlier as he was bound by the secrecy his official position imposed.

The police authorities appreciated his help so much that though he was no longer on the force he had been appointed 'an official expert of criminal telepathy'.

It seemed that before Thoma's regular attachment, these methods were employed only rarely. The first to experiment with it was a French *juge d'instruction* (investigating magistrate) who, while dealing with a murder case, had a number of witnesses hypnotised. One of them, the report said, admitted under hypnosis that he was the murderer and at the same time provided details so that later, in his waking state, when confronted with them he made a full confession. (Such a confession would not have been valid if made under hypnosis.) This caused a considerable commotion among the criminal lawyers who accused the *juge d'instruction* of using force—mental, if not physical—to extract an admission of guilt.

Dr Thoma's methods were entirely different. He did not try to hypnotise any suspects or witnesses. He used a medium who went under the name of Megalis ('Mother of Secrets') and who, in a hypnotic trance, was supposed to 'see' crimes of which she had no previous knowledge.

In June 1921 my father met both Dr Thoma and his medium. He was a middle-aged, distinguished-looking man; she was only eighteen, very thin and frail-looking, pretty, with dark-brown hair and delicate features.

At the first meeting Dr Thoma, now head of the psychological department of the Vienna *Polizeidirektion*, explained that he had been working for many months to harness hypnosis (and through it, telepathy) to the service of criminal investigation. His articles in the Viennese press which he published under the pseudonym 'Tanteauge' had acquired a wide popularity. Though the experiments were still carried out on a very modest scale and he only tackled cases which baffled normal police methods, Thoma achieved more than one success which he maintained could not have been gained by 'normal' means.

'I have been trying for a long time to find a way through which hypnosis-induced telepathy could be employed in criminal investigation,' Dr Thoma told my father. 'But I lacked a suitable medium until I met Miss Megalis who has placed her talents at our disposal during the last twelve months. My starting point was the well-known ability of a hypnotised subject to transfer itself in a state of trance to the past, to places and situations which he or she had never visited or witnessed; to supply descriptions of persons and events which could not be obtained, because of the lack of clues, by ordinary police methods.'

'But is this ability reliable and constant?'

'No, of course not. The useful and valuable results of these trances are sometimes lost in confusion; these results *are* produced by the effects of various factors. The strength of hypnotic clairvoyance depends first of all on whether at the time of the experiment the medium is in a suitable condition for the creation of an intensive nervous reaction. We must never forget that in such a trance the medium does not know that he or she must examine something for the benefit of our investigation; he or she observes with the average interest of a lay person. For instance, such a medium is able to give a more exact description if the criminal is an unusual, extraordinary individual than if he is just a "man-in-the-street". A medium can follow better the path of stolen or lost objects if these have gained his liking or interest. Sometimes quite intelligent and serious mediums make utterances which sound childish.'

He provided a striking example: 'Once when the Warsaw police turned to me in a murder case (it was combined with robbery), I tried to "transfer" Miss Megalis to the scene of the crime. She said in her trance, among other things: "A small shop in a side street. A jeweller's. A little old man sits in the doorway. Two men walk up to him. He ushers them into the shop. He turns his back to them to take something from a shelf. One of the two callers is a short, bald-headed man; he pulls a rubber truncheon from under his coat and hits the jeweller over the head. *I don't like the bald man.* He is an insignificant, antipathetic person. His companion is tall, with an interesting face. He interests me; I watch him. The small man gives the slumped old jeweller three more blows. Then they hurriedly collect the jewellery within reach. Now they walk through the door. In the street they separate. *I am going to follow the man with the striking face . . .*" Then she described the movements of this man—who was only the accomplice, not the murderer—accompanying him to his home, describing the house, the flat . . .'

'Was her vision correct?'

'We notified the Warsaw police at once. As all the data corresponded to the facts, it was easy to track down the second criminal. But in the meantime this accomplice, the "man with the striking face", had joined the Polish army and was captured by the Russians. We do not know what happened to him and the Russians refused to extradite him even when the Russo-Polish war had ended. As Megalis was not "interested" in the murderer himself, it took much longer to arrest him. Clairvoyance can play strange tricks . . .'

Dr Thoma continued: 'However, certain experiments resulted in immediate and complete success. For instance, we discovered the burglar who had robbed the Viennese Union of Cabdrivers and the embezzlers who stole a large amount from a big bank. There have been less important cases in which it was not so much the sum involved or the seriousness of the offence which interested the authorities, but the cunning trickery of the execution. Megalis, for instance, provided useful if incomplete data in some recent attempts at political murders. Thus, the man responsible for the plot to blow up a Cabinet Minister's car near St Egyd was caught partly through her help. It is certainly true that the hypnotic vision of the so-called "bloody" crimes excites and thus dims the medium's abilities. But I hope that soon I'll be able to add hypnosis-induced telepathy to the already numerous methods of criminal investigation and pursuit.'

Less than two months later he and Megalis gave a tangible demonstration of these methods. Within nine days, between 15 and 25 July, four tourists disappeared without trace in the vicinity of Hallstatt in the Austrian Salzkammergut. Hundreds of people searched the neighbourhood but in vain. On 27 July a seventeen-year-old Hungarian student, Charles Ribary, was added to the list of those missing. This led to the definite conclusion that foul play must be involved. The best-trained police dogs were taken to Hallstatt and Ribary's rucksack was found—but no trace of the young man. On 3 August, while the police were still in the district, a sixth young man, a student named Grafeneder, disappeared. Again there was a widespread and thorough search but without the slightest result. The police experts returned to Vienna.

Two days later my father received a telegram from Dr Thoma who had promised that he would let him know if 'something really interesting' cropped up. The *Polizeirat* had offered his services to help find Ribary and the others. *Regierungsrat* Pachta, head of the Salzkammergut police, had welcomed his offer and he was leaving at once for Traunkirchen with Miss Megalis and Herr Platzer, Director of the Viennese Institute of Criminal Telepathy. Would Mr Tabori like to join him?

This was an invitation few crime reporters could resist and my father travelled to Traunkirchen with Dr Géza

Ribary, uncle of the young man who had vanished. They met Dr Thoma and Miss Megalis in Hallstatt.

Later my father wrote the following account of what happened:

'I'm glad you came,' Thoma said. 'Some of your colleagues have been reporting such silly things that I really don't know how to refute them. One said that I had asked fifteen thousand crowns for my services! Dr Ribary can tell you what truth there is in such an allegation.'

'None at all,' Géza Ribary said. 'And I am most grateful to you and Miss Megalis whether you succeed or not. My sister, young Charles's mother, is almost out of her mind with anxiety. If we can bring some certainty to her . . .'

Some rich Viennese bankers who had villas in the neighbourhood had put three automobiles at our disposal. As Miss Megalis got into the first one, she suddenly shuddered and said: 'I am sorry I came . . . I am afraid . . . it will be too exciting . . . I feel frightened.'

Dr Thoma reassured her: 'We must help these people, my dear,' he said. 'You only have to concentrate—and it need not take long.'

We drove down to Marienruh and arrived looking like dusty ghosts. We all got out and Dr Thoma bound the medium's eyes; he said that it would help her to concentrate. Then he said to her: 'It is July thirty-first, a quarter to three in the afternoon. Transfer yourself to that date and tell me what you see.'

'I see nothing,' replied the medium.

'Stay here,' Dr Thoma continued, 'at the same place and time and watch what happens. Tell me what you see now.'

'I see a young man on this spot and a woman with two children.'

'What are they doing?'

'They talk—unimportant things. Later they separate.

The young man goes on alone, climbing; the woman and the two children descend the mountain.'

At this point Dr Thoma awakened the medium from her trance and we all walked uphill in the direction Miss Megalis had indicated in her hypnotic trance. When we reached the crest, he put her into a trance again. Then he said: 'It is July thirty-first, three o'clock. Whom do you see?'

'No one,' replied the medium.

'It is now a quarter past three, July the thirty-first. Tell me exactly what is happening on this spot or around it . . .'

'I see the same young man,' answered the medium, 'who has been talking to the lady and the two children. He is not alone; there are two men in his company. They walk along this path towards the Mühlbach stream . . .'

'Take careful notice of the spot you see now and when I awaken you from your trance, show us exactly where it is. Now tell me what do you see there . . .?'

'They walk towards the stream, all three of them,' replied the medium. 'They start quarrelling and fighting. I have a . . . bad feeling. I am afraid.'

Again Dr Thoma reassured her. 'Do not get excited. It is only make-believe; they are making a motion picture. Tell me what they are doing . . .'

'They fight . . .' the medium began, hesitantly, 'The young man loses his rucksack and his cloak. They go on fighting. One of the strange men takes a square object from the young man's pocket. The young man falls to the ground. His attacker lifts him and places him in the ravine in such a position as if to indicate that he has fallen and killed himself . . . He takes his wrist-watch . . .'

Miss Megalis began to tremble; she was visibly exhausted and suddenly collapsed. Dr Thoma revived her. Lying on the ground, she continued to shiver.

'What is the stranger like?' Dr Thoma asked.

'He is fair-haired, of medium height, and has a moustache,' replied the medium, she then told us the spot where the victim of the murder had been placed—'It is down there,' she pointed, 'but it is a very dangerous spot . . . I am a weak woman, I cannot go down there . . .'

Dr Thoma brought her from her trance. The place she had indicated had been searched thoroughly and in any case it was getting too dark to explore it again. We returned to Hallstatt.

'Well, what do you think?' I asked Dr Ribary.

'I don't know,' he replied thoughtfully, 'much of what she said was remarkable . . .'

'How can you tell that unless you really find your nephew in the spot she indicated?'

'Well, the first thing that struck me was the wrist-watch. We issued a personal description of my nephew which was printed in most papers and widely circulated. However, by some oversight the fact that he was wearing a wrist-watch was omitted. How could Miss Megalis know that he had one? Of course, many people have, but it is a small, circumstantial detail. More important than this is her speaking of a "square object" which was taken from my nephew's pocket. This is really striking for he never carried a wallet or purse; he kept his money in a square note-book. Then again, I checked on that meeting with the woman and the two children. Mrs Maria Lux was the last person to see Charles alive. The newspapers spoke of *three* children being with her and her and she herself thought that this was so. But now we have discovered that she had only her two sons with her, the daughter had stayed at home . . .'

'These are certainly interesting contributions,' I said, 'but nothing conclusive.'

'Would you like to come with me to the Beinkammer?' asked Dr Ribary. 'The police say that my nephew visited it on the day he disappeared.'

'The *Beinkammer*?' I repeated. And then I remembered it was the name of the Hallstatt morgue to which from time to time unidentified bodies, suicides, etc, were taken.

We walked down to the place and found an old woman in charge. Ribary began to question her and discovered that his nephew had been there about two hours before he met Mrs Lux on the mountain path.

'He was a funny one,' the old woman said in her broad Salzkammergut accent. 'He asked me to leave him alone for a moment in this place; he said he wanted to feel "all spooky". I told him I couldn't do that; I was too nervous for such foolery. Then he went away . . .'

'Was he alone?' demanded Dr Ribary.

'Quite alone,' the old woman nodded, 'only . . .'

'Yes?' we both pounced on her and tried to jog her memory. After half an hour's questioning we managed to get something useful and pretty startling out of her. It seemed that a working-class man followed young Ribary and offered to lead him to the finest view of the district, about an hour and a half's distance. But what was even more significant: *the description the old woman gave, tallied in every detail with that of Miss Megalis's vision.*

This gave a strong motivation for us to return early next day to the ravine. We brought some strong rope with us and Dr Thoma himself climbed down, a distance of some two hundred feet. Then he signalled us to follow him which I did with some trepidation for my mountaineering days were far in the past. Under the perpendicular rock-wall we found the opening of a cave. We penetrated several hundred yards into it before we came upon a little underground stream. Here we found a large stone sticking out of the water. It took the three of us to lift it. Ribary's body had been wedged underneath. His belongings had been removed—except, strangely enough, the wrist-watch which had stopped at four o'clock.

A week later, still on the basis of the medium's description, a labourer was arrested and confessed not only to Ribary's murder but to three other killings. His accomplice, a woodcutter, disappeared and was not arrested until almost a year had passed.

Dr Thoma and Megalis were involved in a number of other cases. One of them involved a young girl who was arrested on a charge of fraud; there was no direct proof against her yet she confessed. Dr Thoma proved that this confession was 'suggested' by a police official who shouted at her during the questioning: 'You did it!' This accusation practically hypnotised the young, shy girl—she made her confession in a trance even though she was innocent. Megalis established the real culprit within a couple of days and the young girl was released.

After a whole string of successes, Dr Thoma acquired a formidable reputation and there was hardly anybody who questioned his medium's reliability. This reputation began to have a strange preventive effect—a wallet containing a large sum of money disappeared from the office of a big mining company and the directors called in Dr Thoma; but before he could even start his investigation, an old, high-ranking official of the company called on him, handed over the wallet (with its contents intact) and asked him not to publish his name. It was his son who had stolen it; but when he heard that Megalis was to be consulted, he went to his father and admitted his guilt as he felt that he could not escape discovery.

While the Viennese police co-operated fully with the hypnotist, other experts were more sceptical. What puzzled them was the occult element. How could a young woman, inexperienced and uneducated, describe events of which she could not have had any previous knowledge? Dr Thoma himself was unable to answer these questions; he only applied and utilised the 'still unknown natural forces', comparing himself to a child switching on the light without having any idea about the nature of electricity.

There was nothing about him that would invoke the image of a sinister Svengali. His appearance, his manner, his way of life were anything but 'metaphysical', solemn or pompous. But he was an extraordinary hypnotist who demonstrated his powers by putting into a trance some forty-odd perfectly normal and sane men and women who then performed the usual 'feats'—eating and drinking with splendid gusto non-existent dishes and beverages, handling invisible knives and forks and praising the imaginary banquet.

According to some specialists Dr Thoma's experiments confirmed the teachings of the School of Nancy according to which hypnotic and post-hypnotic suggestion could be used to turn people into criminals. This was, as we have seen before, strongly opposed by other experts, notably the School of Paris which denied these possibilities. Most criminal codes quite explicitly banned hypnosis from being applied either to defendants or to witnesses—on the principle that any testimony must be based on the free, conscious, voluntary action of the individual.

Augusto Agabiti, the Italian psychiatrist, collected several striking cases in the review *Filosofia della Scienza*. Some of these were obvious enough and had their well-accepted parallels in medical experiments using placebos and control groups in testing various treatments and drugs. Professor Slosson of the University of Wyoming conducted a basic, yet striking test. He produced a small bottle in front of his students which contained distilled water. He told his audience, however, that the contents were a strong perfume. He sprinkled a few drops on the desk and asked the students to tell him how long it took them to start smelling the scent. Within fifteen seconds several of the students nearest to the desk lifted their hands to signal that they did so; within forty seconds those farthest away in the large classroom, shaped like an amphitheatre, joined them. About two-thirds of the entire audience ended up by agreeing with the first group—some even found the scent so overpowering that they had to leave.

Suggestibility is not restricted to *outside* influences; it can work, under certain favourable—or malicious—circumstances in the form of auto-suggestion. (This is the basis of at least 90 per cent of the success of faith-healers.) One of the earliest examples observed was the particular sensitivity of pregnant women to different psychological factors. Sixteenth- and seventeenth-century doctors ascribed to the workings of the heightened imagination of expectant women the facial resemblance between the children of the same mother. As a practical extension of this belief aristocratic and royal families decorated the quarters of pregnant women with beautiful paintings and statues in the belief that these would actually influence the features of the unborn child. Naturally, the opposite was believed to be effective, too—any unpleasant or frightening psychical impression would have an unfavourable influence upon the evolution of the foetus.

The Italian alienist Rolfi described some striking examples of the overwhelming power of auto-suggestion in his *Magia Moderna*.

A criminal condemned to death was handed over to some rather unorthodox psychiatric researchers. He was placed on the operating table, told that his main artery was to be opened and that he would slowly bleed to death. His eyes were bandaged, and his neck was pricked with a needle —but lightly, so that it did not even draw blood—and a bottle was placed near his head from which, through a rubber tube, water was slowly emptying, in a thin jet, upon the spot where he had felt the needle's prick. He could hear how the water emptied into a vessel placed on the ground. Within six minutes his heart stopped beating. He believed that his veins had been drained of blood and under this auto-suggestive influence he suffered a cardiac arrest.

(Whether this story is true or not, remains to be established—Rolfi relates it as something that had taken place in one of the southern states of America though his references are somewhat vague. We know, of course, that in our own times convicts have volunteered for dangerous medical experiments, but this particular example appears to belong more to science fiction or a horror story than to actual fact.)

On the other hand a different, equally fatal story was fully reported by an Italian medical review. A young man, suffering from an unhappy love-affair, poisoned himself with mercuric chloride tablets. Though the doctors did everything possible, he died, displaying every symptom of the deadly poison. But the autopsy showed absolutely no trace of mercuric chloride. All they found were slight traces of ordinary kitchen salt. The investigation proved that the chemist where he bought the tablets suspected from his behaviour that he planned suicide—and sold him some salt tablets instead. But he *believed* that he was taking poison, and his body reacted to this intense auto-suggestion.

An aristocratic lady, suffering from what seemed to be incurable kleptomania, specialised in plundering the famous Louvre department store in Paris. Within three months she had stolen two lorry-loads of merchandise. She was caught and the court asked Professor Voisin, the famous alienist, to examine her. The lady, barely twenty, proved to be extremely responsive to hypnosis, and in a hypnotic trance she confessed that she had an accomplice whose overwhelming psychic influence forced her into theft. As most of her loot was returned, she was put on probation and sent to a clinic. After six months she was discharged, apparently cured.

Alfred Pethes

The story of Alfred Pethes, a Hungarian hypnotist who had a distinguished career in aiding the Budapest police, was just as extraordinary as the tally of his various exploits.

He was born into a very poor but musical family and he became an accomplished bassoon-player in the orchestra of the Budapest Royal Opera House. A handsome, slightly plump man with an olive complexion and thick, unruly black hair, he led a quiet, reasonably contented life—until one day he discovered his own powers by a half-ludicrous, half-sinister incident.

He told me the story himself, for in the early thirties we became friends, and I often visited his large and pleasant apartment in the Hungarian capital.

'It was this girl—one of those intense females, big-bosomed, dark-eyed, heavily made-up, her skirt ridiculously short, her jumper a garish purple . . . it is now more than ten years ago but I still remember every detail clearly. We got on the tram together and had to stand close to each other—she was practically in my arms. Her perfume was the worst—a cheap chypre—I couldn't get away from it. She kept chattering all the time, about a party we had both attended about a week ago; about music, clothes, dancing and the latest bestseller. Her mind was as shallow as a pool of rainwater—and almost as muddy. I felt a growing irritation creeping up from my feet, my whole body was prickling with the heat and the desire to get away from her. I was late; the rehearsal had been called for eleven-thirty and it was twenty-five to twelve now . . .'

At last they reached the stop where Pethes had to get off, but to his disgust, the girl followed him. He wanted to hurry away but she took hold of his sleeve and pointed to a huge poster on the corner which announced a performance of 'Professor Leo, the world-famous great phenomenon of will-power'. The red letters screamed against a bilious yellow background:

Some items of Professor Leo's magnificent performance:
The secrets of the holy men of India (an insoluble mystery to all other Europeans to this very day).
Any member of the public can express any desire, wish or longing . . . and it will be fulfilled.
Tell me your secret wish:—
Do you want to be a great actor, dancer, musician, singer?
Do you want to travel—by car, ocean steamer, express train, aeroplane—to exotic lands?
Do you wish to be relieved of your harmful passions—gambling, drinking, smoking, jealousy, etc?
Do you want hair on your bald pate, new teeth in your mouth, youth to replace senility?
Do you wish to roam in the domain of miraculous visions and hallucinations?
There is no human dream, ideal or wish which a single magic glance of the Great Master cannot turn into reality!

While the girl was reading the garish lines aloud, the young bassoon-player was desperately trying to get away without being rude—but she clung to him like a leech. When he called the great professor a 'cheap trickster', she replied that she'd love to be hypnotised herself, she just *knew* she was a perfect medium. Then she added: 'You know, I am sure you would make an awfully good hypnotist. You have such big black eyes . . . they are glowing and burning. I think that if you told me that I couldn't move an inch . . . I . . . I would instantly obey and . . .'

Pethes lost his patience. He gave her a look of utter

contempt and almost shouted: 'All right . . . you can't move . . . not an inch . . .'

Her mouth gaped; she seemed unable to close it. Her body was half-turned, her legs planted sturdily and squarely on the hot pavement. Not a muscle twitched. The silly cow, the bassoonist thought, now she's play-acting, wasting my time. He would be fined for being late—maybe even sacked.

He began to urge her: 'Come on, now. I'm afraid I must go. Hope to see you next week . . .'

Slowly, painfully, her lips moved. With an immense effort she articulated the words: 'I . . . I . . . can't move . . .'

Pethes got furious. He had no time for such stupid jokes . . . And then his heart missed a beat. For the girl's whole body was straining, half aslant . . . and yet she did not fall. She was held rigid as if in a vice. Her face twisted in fear. She *was* actually in some kind of trance.

He heard laughter and turned to see half-a-dozen people staring at them. 'One of these Svengalis,' he heard a thin young man say. Sweating, he turned back to the girl. 'Come on, relax,' he urged, 'try it slowly . . . I don't want you to stay like this. I want you to move . . . I command you . . .'

A moment later a policeman arrived and demanded to know what was going on. Pethes tried to explain that the young lady was feeling the heat, that everything would be all right. The policeman made the crowd disperse. But the girl was still completely rigid.

He touched her arm. It was icy cold, in spite of the heat. He remembered something he had read in an article and stroked her forehead, passing his fingers over her eyes. And suddenly, just as the policeman was fumbling for his notebook, she relaxed, shook herself and smiled at him. 'Why, that was wonderful . . . I don't quite know what happened . . . but I feel so cool and rested . . .'

Pethes fled, without even saying goodbye.

He would have been only too happy to forget the whole incident, but the girl blabbed and, unfortunately, they moved in the same middle-class circles, went to the same parties, visited the same swimming-pools and cheap dance halls. He was a young man without a family, his parents had died, the few relatives left were mostly living in Slovakia; he could not suddenly withdraw. So he had to endure the banter and the rather vulgar interest aroused by the girl's tales. At the parties he was forced to play the part of the 'hypnotist', and somehow, he felt a strange power flooding his whole being, flowing out of him and then ebbing. There were the usual silly tricks; making someone drink a glass of water in the belief that it was brandy; turning a young female body into a rigid bridge between two chairs; sending ordinary young men into poetic raptures over the charms of a particularly ugly old woman—parlour games, childish entertainment which he hated afterwards. Yet the queer flood and flow of power was there, and once or twice when he failed, he felt angry and bewildered.

One night, after a particularly hilarious session, a tall man with horn-rimmed spectacles and sandy hair came up to him and introduced himself as Dr V, a psychiatrist. He had been sitting for most of the evening in a corner, toying with a single drink and smoking expensive cigars. He told Pethes that he was interested in his performance; would he visit him at his home as they might have 'many things to discuss'. Pethes, wilfully misunderstanding him, asked whether Dr V was interested in music.

'Not particularly,' the doctor smiled, 'but I'm interested in you and in your remarkable powers. Do come and see me one day next week.'

And when Pethes did go—mostly out of curiosity—he

found that the doctor had a spotless surgery, an efficient-looking secretary and a general air of affluence. When they were alone, he came straight to the point: 'Would you be interested in changing your profession, Mr Pethes?'

The bassoon-player replied that he didn't quite understand.

'It's very simple,' Dr V continued, 'I'm a psychiatrist. People come to me with their mental and physical ailments, and I try to cure them—sometimes by hypnotism. I have studied the technique in Paris and Brussels. But unfortunately I have not the power, the concentrated strength of suggestion. With me, it is a hit-and-miss affair . . . with you, I can see, it is a constant flowing strength, and hypnotism, in spite of the stupid bunk written and talked about it, is a great healing power if rightly handled. We cannot cure cancer by hypnotism but we can cure almost any nervous disease, bad habit, or non-organic trouble.

Pethes replied that this was all very interesting but he couldn't see what it had to do with him. Dr V smiled.

'How would you like to earn ten . . . twenty . . . fifty times as much as you are earning now?' he asked. 'Well, you could—easily—if you joined me. Together we would make a wonderful team. The success of a single cure would attract fifty other patients. There is a growing tendency to become involved with the occult, with various semi-scientific and utterly bogus movements. Theosophy, spiritualism, all the cults—they flower after every war, every great disaster. But we wouldn't bother with ghosts or spirit writing. I'm a fully qualified physician—you could become my assistant. I would cover all expenses and give you 30 per cent of the net profits. What do you say?'

After wrestling for two weeks with his conscience, the bassoon-player accepted Dr V's offer. They did not put their agreement into writing—the doctor said that a gentleman's word was good enough and after all, it was to their mutual interest that they should continue to collaborate and Pethes was too young, too much impressed by the doctor's polished manners and evident affluence to insist upon it. He had a good many things to learn. His new partner gave him books and delivered long lectures on the 'psychological pre-treatment of patients'. He was a superb salesman and his bedside manner one of the suavest. Three months after Alfred Pethes had joined him, Dr V began to insert discreet announcements in the daily papers about hypnotic cures and individual treatment of all nervous disorders—a practice which contemporary medical ethics found quite permissible.

Soon people were flocking to the villa near the town park where Dr V had installed his new consulting rooms. Most of the patients were women, but a little later harassed tycoons, inhibited politicians, slightly unbalanced civil servants all mingled with the hysterical females. The majority of their ailments were imaginary and therefore the easier to cure. But by the end of the first year some of the big hospitals and private nursing homes started to send them their most serious cases. Though he was getting rather cynical and hard-boiled about his new profession, Pethes could not help feeling a deep excitement when he succeeded in making a giant of six foot six walk for the first time after five years of nervous paralysis. It was the power flowing from him that roused the huge man from his wheelchair, made him throw away his crutches and, faltering, swaying, walk a few steps. He was a former captain in a Hussar regiment who had become a cripple through shell-shock. Organically there was little wrong with him; yet his rigid nerves had to be untangled and relaxed in hypnotic sleep until, after many painstaking treatments, he was completely recovered.

In the beginning Dr V was always present but when he

saw that his partner was picking up the jargon, the polished manner, he spent less and less time in the consulting rooms. Pethes overheard a stray remark which did not strike him as very important—evidently the doctor had one passion, gambling, which took up a good deal of his days. He was also developing political ambitions; there was some talk that he would stand for parliament at the next elections. All this interested his partner little, for work absorbed him more and more. His somewhat raucous voice became deep and soft; he learned how to dress with unassuming elegance. Most of the patients he treated were well-to-do, cultured, interesting; they all bared their souls to him and sometimes he felt like a father-confessor. There seemed to be no limit to his inherent power; sometimes, after a tiring day, he faced his mirror and could calm himself down with the tonic he supplied so lavishly to others.

He made plenty of money and could spend it on himself. He went to concerts, bought himself the finest bassoon he could find; once every six months he took a fortnight's holiday. The books Dr V gave him to read awakened his interest in psychology and the psychic sciences, and he attended séances although he did not believe in any of the phenomena, knowing that the force within his own comfortable, plump body was tangible proof of the existence of things unseen and inexplicable.

By the end of the year he was absolutely sure of himself. Dr V was hardly ever seen at the villa; he had stood for parliament and won with a handsome majority. Everything seemed to be perfect in the garden though in the last two or three months Alfred's share in the 'business' seemed to decrease steadily. He tried to question his partner about this but could never pin him down. Still, the money was quite enough for his modest needs and his interest in his work became keener every day.

Then he fell in love with a singer whose great problem had been stage-fright—which Pethes cured in less than a dozen sessions. To court her, he needed money—more than he was making. He bearded Dr V again but the suave psychiatrist was not very helpful. Pethes managed to get hold of the books by bribing the accountant who kept them, and discovered that the doctor had been cheating him of considerable amounts, paying him far less than was due to him.

His infatuation with the singer egged him on; there was a stormy scene of recrimination. But Dr V was perfectly self-assured. They had no written agreement, had they? He had made Alfred Pethes what he was and could undo his work whenever he wanted.

This raised the fighting spirit of the ex-bassoon-player. He damned Dr V and told him that they were through; he could start a business of his own whereas the doctor was helpless without him. But Dr V said that his good friend was mistaken—he had decided to give up medicine and go in for a purely political career. One of the bills he had tabled for early discussion (and he had the necessary support) would ban anyone except a fully qualified doctor from administering hypnotic treatment. He could get an assistant any time—and in case Alfred Pethes changed his mind, *he* would not . . . he needn't come in any more.

The same evening the young man poured all his troubles into the singer's small ears. He expected encouragement, commiseration, sympathy—but she stared at him and said: 'What an impractical man you are!' Two days later when he came to her hotel he was told that she had left, without a forwarding address.

The bill disqualifying anyone except doctors from hypnotic practice was duly passed, and Alfred Pethes was a law-abiding man. For the first time in two-and-a-half-years he took stock of his material and spiritual assets and found them slender enough. Yet he did not despair. He was cured of his infatuation; but he was grimly resolved to get his own back on Dr V. There seemed to be only one way of doing it—he must become a doctor himself.

He was almost thirty and also a Jew. They laughed when he enquired about the possibilities of enrolling at the medical faculty of Budapest University. The semi-fascist, feudal government's *numerus clausus* restricted the number of Jewish students to 5 per cent of the total—and these places were more or less reserved for the influential and the rich. He did not even have a high school diploma; his schooling had ended when he was fourteen.

He had very little money saved, but he carefully worked out a budget and went back to school. He passed the necessary secondary school examinations in a year—competing with fifteen-, sixteen- and seventeen-year-olds in succession. Then he went through the *matura*, which embraced the material of eight years of high school. Yet he was still far from his goal; no Hungarian university would admit him and he had no money left.

He arrived in Vienna with a small suitcase, a few schillings in his pockets and the same dogged, grim determination. The first year at the university was a nightmare. At thirty-one the mind is not as supple and quick as at eighteen or nineteen which was the average age of his fellow-students. But he did not falter. Then, at the end of the second year, he ran into Armin Silverman, the great art dealer who had once met him in Budapest, a hard, harsh man who had one weak spot: a twelve-year-old daughter. Clara was a lovely child but a shock in her early childhood had deprived her of the ability to speak. Dozens of specialists had tried to cure her, in vain. Silverman decided on a last desperate experiment and when the university's long vacation started, he rented a villa in Mödling and installed Clara, a nurse and Alfred Pethes in it.

For three long, hot months Pethes battled with the deeply rooted nervous paralysis of the young girl. Sometimes he was on the verge of giving up the struggle, it seemed hopeless. But he remembered Dr V, and even when he forgot him there were other incentives. He had discovered a deep love of medicine in himself; he had found his true vocation. In the end he was triumphant. Clara Silverman started to speak and soon her speech was quite normal with only occasional odd hesitations, much less than an ordinary stammer.

The great art dealer had more money than he could spend and his gratitude was almost embarrassing. He offered a life-long pension to Pethes, but the hopeful medical student refused. Yet Silverman insisted that he should accept help and bought and equipped a small private nursing home for him on the Semmering. He had no more financial worries; he could have given up his university career but that was the thing farthest from his mind.

It was about this time that he began to work with the Austrian police—perhaps because he wanted to safeguard his own, slightly irregular status, perhaps because he felt a genuine need for public service. Unlike Dr Thoma who had his Megalis, Alfred Pethes was his own medium—a hypnotist who was also a psychic.

One of his most striking cases began when a young woman was brought into the emergency ward of a famous Viennese hospital. She was in a coma and the doctors tried for several hours in vain to restore her to consciousness. It took the police and the ambulance service a long time before they established her identity: she was the wife of a famous pianist, had been married for six years and had two children. It was discovered that she had taken poison in a hysterical fit—more than twenty-five grammes of quinine, dissolved in water. As soon as this fact became known, they used a stomach pump and gave her various antidotes, but though she came out of her coma she suffered one hysterical attack after the other. It was impossible to tell the origin of these violent attacks or find a motive for her suicide attempt. Even while she was unconscious, she kept on screaming and pleading that no doctor should be allowed to come near her —when she was touched, she began to heave and kick, claw and struggle so that the physicians had to tie her to the bed to examine her. In the meantime her husband and a young man in his early twenties, looking very distressed, were standing in the hospital corridor, tensely awaiting the result of the emergency treatment.

Though she left no note, it was obvious that she had been preparing her suicide attempt for several days. She went the round of several chemists to obtain quinine, dissolved it in water and kept the glass on her bedside table—until the moment when, apparently, she took the final decision to kill herself.

After two days the doctors succeeded in saving her life and restoring her to at least a semblance of normality. A week later she was discharged. But as soon as she got home, her hysterics recommenced. She had terrible fits of rage and a family friend suggested to the husband that he should take her to a psychiatrist.

The pianist was a friend of Armin Silverman, and so he came to Pethes. The hypnotist asked him to bring his wife along—she was now sufficiently recovered to go out though still subject to her mysterious fits of rage. Next afternoon the three of them called—the lady, her husband and the rather strange-looking young man who declared that as a friend of the family he would not leave the couple even for a moment. When the young woman found out where she was, she went into hysterics again and started to scream:

'I won't be touched, I won't be hypnotised! I was told to stay away from any such mumbo-jumbo. Leave me alone —or I'll jump from the window . . .'

Pethes managed to calm her, at least temporarily. It did not take him long to discover that she *was* in a hypnotic trance, that her hysterics had the same origin, and that her suicide attempt was also due to it. Someone had suggested to her that she was hopelessly, tragically in love and that she had no choice but to die.

But as Pethes continued his exploration, he came to another, even more striking conclusion. The husband, too, was under hypnosis. He had absorbed the suggestion that he and his family had only one true friend and support—the peculiar-looking young man who had accompanied them to Pethes as a selfless and benevolent associate.

Pethes immediately sent for a doctor friend of his who gave this couple the proper treatment, but he did not permit the young man to leave. It turned out that he was a violinist appearing in a rather sleazy nightclub. There was a long and tense confrontation; finally a sad and extraordinary family tragedy was unveiled.

The twenty-two-year-old young man had made the pianist's acquaintance about two years before. The young wife had been suffering from a bilious complaint. The young man told her that he had attended some hypnotic séances where healing sessions were held, people were relieved of headaches and toothaches—he undertook to use the same method to rid the lady of her painful attacks.

She proved to be a submissive medium and he did succeed in alleviating her pain.

He used this success for hypnotising the young wife regularly—and suggesting to her that she was in love with *him*. She accepted this totally but it seemed that the situation gradually became uncomfortable for the young man and so he hypnotised her again, telling her that she could not live without him and if he left her, she would poison herself.

But even this was not sufficient for the budding Svengali. Now he turned to the husband, hypnotised him and suggested to him that he, the pianist, must plead with the amateur hypnotist to entertain his wife, to look after her 'as the only true and reliable friend of the family'.

On top of all this he gave a hypnotic command to the wife never to allow a doctor to come near her, and to protest violently against any examination or attempted cure. For almost two years she obeyed this cruel command until her nervous system was totally disrupted and she became the prey of a rising hysteria. Then, after a violent quarrel when she discovered that the young man wanted to leave her, she prepared her suicide systematically and finally made the attempt.

Freed from their hypnotic obsessions by Pethes, the pianist and the young wife gave a good many other details; it turned out that they were not the only victims of the unscrupulous nightclub violinist. He apparently used his hypnotic powers to seduce a number of women—and men, for it was established that he was bisexual. In the following months Pethes treated almost a dozen of these and gradually freed them from their total dependence on the scoundrel—who was later tried and sentenced to three years in prison.

It was through one of his police cases—the unmasking of a particularly vicious blackmailer whose numerous victims refused to testify against him until Pethes removed this 'block' by hypnotism—that the former basoonist met Elsa, a young pianist. They were married within five weeks of their first meeting and their happiness seemed to be complete. Two boys were born in the first three years of their marriage, and Alfred Pethes proved his mastery of mind over matter when he put his wife into a trance so that she bore her children without an anaesthetic and without pain. By the time the older boy was three, Pethes had passed his finals in Vienna and received his degree. He was fully qualified; now he could have his revenge on Dr V which he was not prepared to forego.

Yet perhaps he would have stayed in Vienna if Silverman had not suffered grave losses in 1929 when the bottom fell out of world economy and the price of art treasures slumped. The nursing home on the Semmering gave treatment to poor and rich alike—but now the rich seemed to disappear. Silverman offered to continue backing Pethes but the young doctor refused. He felt sufficiently confident to stand on his own feet. So next spring he moved his family to Budapest; he had saved enough money to set himself up and with Elsa's help he created a lovely home in a quiet Buda street.

But his difficulties were not yet over. Though he had acquired a doctor's degree in Vienna, this did not entitle him, he discovered, to practise in Hungary. Doctors all over Europe were organised in guilds and societies which looked upon a foreign intruder as upon a dangerous enemy. When Alfred Pethes was told this by his solicitor, he grew pale. Elsa, who accompanied him everywhere, pressed his hand. 'Perhaps we'd better go back to Vienna,' she murmured.

'No!' he almost shouted. 'We are staying here.'

From that day on he deliberately broke the law a dozen times every twenty-four hours, but as his patients included high civil servants, police officers and aristocrats, he had no trouble in carrying on his practice as a psychiatrist. He was consulted almost weekly by detectives and investigating magistrates; he helped to clear up more than a hundred particularly difficult cases in the early thirties. At the same time he had once more enrolled as a student and was passing the examinations which Hungarian law prescribed for doctors with a foreign degree. Two more years—and then nothing could stand in his way.

The two years passed. He was handed his diploma, the magic key which would open the last locked door. Everything was perfect—until, in the late thirties, the anti-Jewish laws of Nazi Germany were gradually introduced into Hungary. Once again Pethes was banned from his vocation, his true mission. And one day in 1941 he walked from his apartment, sat down on a bench in a secluded part of the town park and shot himself.

Dr V, however, survived. He lent his talents to the Gestapo to extract confessions from stubborn prisoners. And when the communist regime was installed in Hungary, he did the same work for the new masters. Several people who escaped after the 1956 Revolution spoke of the tall, bland man who devised and carried out the most refined psychological torture to break their spirits and extract confessions. He died in the early sixties, still exploiting unscrupulously the weakness of human-beings and the powers which he himself possessed.

Mittelmann and Richard

There have been, of course, a good many others who used hypnosis to aid or conduct criminal investigation.

One of the most amusing practitioners was himself a criminal. In 1931 a trickster named Georg Mittelmann was arrested in Berlin and taken to the Moabit Prison to await questioning. His most recent exploit was to make a bank messenger believe that with the 180,000 marks entrusted to him he would be able to buy dollars at a low price and sell them at a considerable profit—which they would share. He took his inexperienced and rather naive victim to a café, relieved him of the money—saying that he would be back with the large profits within fifteen minutes—and then disappeared through the kitchen. A few days later, however, he was arrested in Marburg and brought to Berlin.

Mittelmann was an experienced amateur hypnotist who used his gifts in various ways; now and then he even aided the police, in order to build up a little store of goodwill for his next encounter with the law. For several months he was employed in a large hardware shop where there were numerous thefts. Mittelmann knew that one of the store-keepers, a man called Johann Salmer, was the prime suspect, but the detectives were unable to prove anything. Mittelmann put Salmer into a hypnotic trance and obtained a confession from him—including the name of the 'fence', a toolmaker named Sepp Kline. Most of the stolen goods were actually found in Kline's house. This success emboldened Mittelmann and he toured several German cities, organising hypnotic séances. But as he had no licence to give such performances, he was fined and forcibly returned to Berlin, his home-town.

When he was arrested because of the theft of the 180,000 marks, he was put into a large cell with several other suspects. The policeman outside the cell suddenly realised that the inventive crook was making a postman (arrested for theft) dance. The lanky, round-faced fellow was gyrating and pirouetting with passionate abandon and performing the most complicated steps, accompanied by the loud laughter of his fellow-prisoners. Detectives and policemen rushed into the cell. In the meantime the hypnotist went to work on a currency smuggler. Within a few seconds he was in a hypnotic trance. Mittelmann made him drink some water and then suggested to him that he had just swallowed a strong aperient. A third prisoner became so drunk from a few drops of water that he attacked the others in sheer high spirits. Mittelmann made an old burglar believe that he was a cat—the old man obediently started to walk on all fours and miaouwed plaintively. Another thief was transformed into a dog whereupon he began to chase 'the cat' on his hands and knees and there would have been a serious fight if the policeman hadn't intervened. When the amateur hypnotist attempted to make some of the suspects confess to crimes which they denied having committed, he was stopped by the detectives who knew only too well that such confessions were not admissible under law. Mittelmann was separated from the rest of the prisoners and was kept under close supervision—but a few days later he escaped and was never found again.

Paul Richard, an investigating magistrate of the small French town of Tulle (Corrèze), was extremely anxious to solve the secret of a plague of anonymous letters. These kept arriving almost daily at various addresses and had led to several suicides and a number of family tragedies. A reward of 50,000 francs was offered; detectives arrived from the Sûreté in Paris to help the local police; all in vain. When the details of the reward were published, Monsieur Richard himself received an anonymous letter with 500 francs enclosed: 'I feel it my duty to add my contribution—and I hope that the miscreant will be soon found. Or perhaps he won't. I'll be interested to watch and see . . .'

Paul Richard added the 500 francs to the 50,000 already deposited; uneasily, he felt that perhaps the donor had a more than charitable interest in the outcome of the investigation. In any case, as he made absolutely no progress, he decided on using unorthodox methods. He asked permission from the Ministry of Interior to employ a hypnotist. Before long Monsieur Thieville, a famous practitioner of the art, arrived in Tulle. The three main suspects—all of them women—were summoned to the magistrate's office, the interior of which had been made spooky by the dimming of the lights. Darkened, with a couple of occult eerie pictures on the wall, and a single guttering candle. It was the proper setting for a séance.

The first suspect was an elegantly dressed lady of about thirty, wife of a high police official.

The magistrate gave her a curt order to be seated. The lady grew pale and obeyed. The hypnotist began his work and soon put her into a trance. Monsieur Richard began the questioning, in the same harsh, commanding tone.

'Who wrote the anonymous letters? You must answer me . . . now!'

The lady sighed, groaned, evidently struggling with some inner block. But finally she replied, in a barely audible voice: 'I . . . I don't know . . .'

The magistrate continued his questioning. Under what circumstances were the letters written? Were there any copies made? Why were certain victims chosen? But the answer was always a barely audible 'I don't know.'

The second suspect, an elderly woman, resisted the hypnotist's efforts—she did not go into a trance and he had to give up the attempt. 'She has a very strong will,' he explained, 'and she refuses to concentrate . . .'

The third subject was a very attractive young woman, a luscious blonde, blue-eyed and with a perfect complexion. The hypnotist had hardly looked at her, when her long lashes began to quiver, her eyelids closed and she fell back in her chair. It was obvious that she would prove a perfect medium. But as the magistrate began to question her, it became evident that she was undergoing considerable strain. Her lips trembled, her whole body quivered.

'Please . . . wake me up . . . I'm suffering . . . terribly. Please, wake me up . . .'

The police officials were startled by her evident anguish

but Monsieur Richard continued: 'Who wrote those anonymous letters . . . you must tell me!'

The girl strained and heaved and repeated: 'Please wake me up . . . I'm in pain . . . great pain . . .'

Though the magistrate went on with his questions, she did not respond, except with repeated pleas to be released from the 'bondage'. In the end the hypnotist woke her from her trance.

Two days later the young girl's *mother* confessed to the authorship of the anonymous letters—and Monsieur Richard had achieved his purpose. Obviously the girl knew of her mother's strange aberration (the lady had reached the menopause and was deeply disturbed in her mind) but could not bring herself to betray her.

Yet the hypnosis served the purpose of the somewhat unscrupulous *juge d'instruction* because the daughter's distress and suffering led to her mother's confession.

Medical and Legal Views

Such developments, however, are rare enough. As Professor Langen has pointed out if in a waking or half-waking state of consciousness a person receives suggestions which do not correspond to the subjective or objective conceptions and attitudes of his ego, the hypnotic condition is removed, 'exploded'. The reactions are usually unease and fear—or simply a deeper level of sleep, followed by spontaneous awakening and the refusal to obey the commands of the hypnotist. The inhibiting effect of the 'super-ego', essentially identical with what we call 'conscience', represents the strongest force which does not permit such an interior influence to work.

The hypnotic condition is also broken when someone

commands the subject to endure or condone a criminal action. If this does NOT happen, generally speaking no hypnosis would have been needed to make someone carry out such action.

On the whole, the hypnotised subject will do everything for the hypnotist as long as his 'super-ego', his conscience, is in harmony with the commands and taboos of his psychological make-up. It is this conscience which has a lasting control over all conscious and unconscious actions and attitudes. Should the hypnotised person go against his ethical norms and values, he is seized by such a strange anxiety ('pangs of conscience') which breaks the hypnotic condition.

We have spoken of a number of experiments which attempted to make people carry out criminal actions under hypnosis—actions that were alien to their waking personalities. Dr L. Mayer in Heidelberg conducted wide-ranging tests on which he reported in his *Das Verbrechen in Hypnose und seine Aufklärungsmethoden* (Crime under Hypnosis and Its Methods of Evaluation) (Munich, 1937). Professor Stockvis of Leyden had done the same in two major works, *Hypnose in der ärztlichen Praxis* (Hypnotism in Medical Practice) (Basle, 1955) and (together with M. Pflanz), *Suggestion in ihrer relativen Betrifflichkeit, medizinisch und sozialpsychologisch betrachtet* (Suggestion in Its Relative Sense, Considered Medically and Socio-Psychologically) (Stuttgart, 1961). M. H. Erikson has described advanced techniques of hypnosis and therapy in the United States and J. G. Watkins explored the transference aspects of hypnotic relationship, publishing a long paper on it in Kline's *Clinical Correlations of Experimental Hypnosis* (1965). The work of all these eminent experts established certain basic points about the possibility of crimes committed under hypnotic influence. Firstly: however carefully and ingeniously these experiments are devised, for the subject they must always remain *recognisably* experiments—and thereby quite clearly distinguishable from reality. Secondly: many factors which are decisive in hypnotism must be looked on as 'playing a part'. The central physiological functions, the ability of criticism and judgement, the exercise of willpower, sensual experiences, the functioning of conscience and the striving to follow norms and rules of accepted human behaviour all remain largely intact in a hypnotic trance. Thirdly: the structure of the subject's personality is far more decisive for the overall happenings in hypnotism than the suggestions given or the so-called 'suggestive power' which is supposed to emanate from the hypnotist. Concerning the suggestion of criminal acts, this means that the carrying-out of these suggestions depends far more on the structure of the medium's personality than on the suggestions and the approach to actuality which these suggestions achieve.

All hypnotic experiments, Professor Langen and his colleagues maintain, prove that *the subject's personality cannot be extinguished*. In all stages of hypnotic trance—even if the rather problematic claim of so-called 'deep hypnosis' is accepted—the subject retains the option to act on his own, spontaneously and freely.

We have described a few cases in which hypnotism has been used for clearing up mysterious crimes, finding the criminal. Most of these belong to the 1920s or the early 1930s. Since then most civilised countries have banned the use of hypnotism (or other means which alter consciousness, such as drugs, etc) in forensic procedures.

In Western Germany (the Federal Republic) Paragraph 136a of the criminal code declares:

'The freedom of voluntary decision and the exercise of the will of the accused must not be impaired by mistreatment, exhaustion, physical intervention, narcotics and other drugs, torture, deceit or hypnotism . . .'

The corresponding paragraph in the Austrian criminal code (*Strafprozessordnung*) says that an accused must not be forced into making a statement or confession either by promises or threats, by deception or forcible means. Though hypnotism is not expressly mentioned, in practice today it is also banned.

In Switzerland hypnotism is not mentioned in the twenty-five different criminal codes regulating police procedure (each canton has a different one) but it is covered under 'forcible means' or 'restriction of voluntary decision', both of which are forbidden to be used.

The Dutch criminal code also contains a paragraph which obliges the investigating magistrate to avoid any measures that 'hinder the free expression of a suspect's or accused's will'.

In the United States both federal and state law contains numerous provisions—some of which have been rephrased or clarified by Supreme Court decisions—protecting the individual rights of prisoners and suspects. The employment of the so-called 'truth drug' (scopomaline) or the lie-detector must never be enforced though the suspect can voluntarily submit to them—provided the legal safeguards are observed. Hypnosis is placed in the same category.

The above procedural and legal provisions are applicable also when someone submits voluntarily to hypnosis. There is a straightforward psychological explanation for this attitude. If an accused person is willing to make a statement, there is no need to put him into a hypnotic trance. Should he want to hide or suppress something, he is not going to submit voluntarily to a hypnotic trance. Finally, it must be remembered that under hypnosis quite fictitious thoughts, fantasies or untruths can be produced just as easily as in a waking state.

However, modern medical science denies any reduced or

removed responsibility of the hypnotised. Hypnosis does not mean a pathologically changed state or disturbance of consciousness. Even though he feels less responsible in a trance, such a subject is always fully responsible under criminal law, because while the state of consciousness might be lowered and restricted, there is only a quantitative change or shifting of the normal conditions, not a qualitative alteration.

Narcotics, psychedelic drugs, alcohol, epilepsy all create serious disturbances of the consciousness and seriously impair memory. In these cases, however, it is quite impossible to restore it, while the hypnotically induced amnesia can always be cured by the appropriate suggestion.

Svengali's heirs can do a good deal of good by curing pathological conditions—but the favourite plot element of Gothic or neo-Gothic novels is pure fiction. Hypnotism can be employed in police investigation, under proper safeguards and with the consent of the suspect or witness involved—but the results are unlikely to be admitted in evidence unless the testimony or confession is repeated in a waking state and under the proper conditions demanded by the law. Of course, there may be countries in which the rights of the accused are less than scrupulously respected—and here the hypnotist who is prepared to abuse and prostitute his powers can still operate and even reap rich rewards.

2
BY THEIR OWN HANDS

Some years ago I watched a graphological experiment which was a startling demonstration of individuality. A young girl, perfectly healthy in body and mind, of an upper-middle-class family was hypnotised and told to write as if she had become a whole series of different people: a man engaged in heavy manual work; a miser; a happy extrovert; a melancholy introvert; a seventy-year-old woman; a first-grade schoolboy. Not only did the girl's facial expressions and gestures change under such suggestion but her handwriting mirrored each character perfectly. Each sample was completely different and none resembled her normal writing.

Among all the movements of the hand, writing is distinguished by the delicacy and precision it demands. It is easy to understand that it led to the development of an independent science, that of graphology. The forms of expression which manifest themselves in handwriting can be regarded as a special kind of natural and unintended gesture.

Examining the often brilliant attempts which graphology makes to analyse and establish the meaning of handwriting, we must remember that the individual peculiarities of the hand movements involved can be measured far more clearly than those of other movements. In writing, people always keep in view the basic forms of letters prescribed by the alphabet—putting on paper the letter 'o', they will try to draw a miniature circle or, in the case of an 'l', to make a loop. We know the general model which individual handwriting is obliged to follow more or less closely to prevent total illegibility. The hand movements in writing differ from all others because of the considerable part thought and emotion play in them—for we write in order to communicate our ideas and feelings. Finally, we know that in the brain the nervous centre of writing is very close to the centres of thought and emotion and is even intimately linked with them. In principle one should be able to form conclusions as to a man's psychological life from *all* movements—his walk or his handshake—but handwriting provides far more lasting and varied clues.

How reliable these clues are has been a subject of considerable argument. The psychologists and philologists who have explored the vast subject have included such serious and responsible people as Michon, Crépieux-Jamin, Preyer and, more recently, Klages (the 'Kant' of graphology), Saudek, Pulver and Jacoby. It is now generally accepted that graphology (though not necessarily every graphologist) is able to identify specific features of the human personality 'with a high degree of reliability'. This needs close analysis of the individual handwriting and considerable care in its interpretation. Firmness, resistance, perseverance, a compassionate disposition and indifference are deduced from the regularity and general character (which Klages calls *Formniveau*, form-level) of the script. The factors on which interpretation is based can be read directly from the writing, but also perceived intuitively (the so-called psychographology with which we are here mainly concerned). Professor Révész, in his *The Human Hand* (1958), says: 'When we consider how swiftly the hand responds to inner excitations and with what delicacy of feeling it can, for example, transmit the feeling-tone of a musical composition to an instrument, it need not seem surprising that handwriting possesses a psychodiagnostic value, which can only be employed, however, in conjunction with other psychological techniques of diagnosis.'

Handwriting consists of thousands of elements. This is a surprising number but individual script can have a great many differing characteristics. Take, for instance, the relative position of the lines. Some people hardly leave any space between them—others a whole finger's breadth. The lines can be horizontal or slanting, parallel or divergent, of equal length or varied, longer on the left or the right side; there are handwritings in which the lines are at first very tightly spaced while later this space widens—or it can be the other way round. As far as the general picture of the lines is concerned, about a hundred different types can be distinguished. Not to mention the position of the individual words; they can be straight or crooked, of equal size, growing or diminishing; the strokes can thicken or thin out; the syllables, the single letters all have their tales to tell. Graphologists have even analysed the *manu propria*—the writing of illiterates, the cross or other sign they make instead of a proper signature.

Another problem of graphology is left-handed writing. By this the experts primarily mean the right-handed writing of left-handed people. If the left-handed are trained to use their right increasingly (naturally, without the ill effects which such a training can cause), conscious practice can develop this manual skill to a normal extent. But in the execution of more delicate movements left-handedness is the source of motional impulses opposed to the organism of the right-handed; this inhibiting effect can be clearly observed in left-handed people writing with the right hand. This is primarily expressed by the handwriting slanting to the left, like mirror writing, while normal writing will always slant to the right, the strokes pointing in the regular, normal direction.

Graphologists had a hard struggle to prove that their profession was a science and not mystical, occult speculation. Yet as an outstanding European expert wrote: 'Graphology uses scientific methods, employing laws which have been checked both practically and theoretically. All you need to be a graphologist is to have a good visual memory, a sound power of observation, a practical knowledge of psychology, and a fair judgment of people. If you possess these qualities or are able to develop them, you, too, can be a graphologist. Of course not by taking some graphological formulae and simply forcing a handwriting into their patterns. All handwritings, like all minds, have their individuality. You have to establish their peculiarities and judge them, within the general laws, according to their separate, special qualities.'

For effective analysis graphologists need 'natural' writing —that is, a script without any compulsion or conscious attempt at legibility or 'beauty'. The sample must have been written without the writer thinking at all about the letters and their shape—but concentrating entirely upon his thoughts, the ideas he wanted to express.

Handwriting can also provide reliable clues to mental or physical illness. This aspect of graphology has been explored by such medical pioneers as Erlenmeyer, G. Meyer, Crépieux-Janin, Preyer and Haarer; Charcot, the brilliant head of the Paris Salpetrière, one of the earliest champions of hypnosis in medicine, also worked in this field. Another French physician, Dr Duparchy-Jeannes, used graphological diagnosis in more than a thousand cases, and according to a carefully prepared report, almost all of these were confirmed by subsequent pathological tests.

All this, however, is not yet sufficient to establish the interrelations, nor even the fact as to whether any abnormality of the organism is manifested to a larger extent in handwriting than in the other expressive movements: gestures, facial expressions or speech.

It is, of course, easy to demonstrate that physical and psychological factors *do* influence handwriting. The slightest indisposition changes our writing to some extent; a serious illness leaves considerable traces. This is because illness usually means the reduction of the vital energy which is expressed by movement.

The general temper of a sick man is less balanced than a normal person's; it can swing between the extremes of depression and excitement, melancholy and irritation. A serious depression involves a decline in movement. Letters become smaller, the speed and pressure of writing decrease, lines become thinner and sometimes lose their definition almost to the point of illegibility. The terminal lines of the words and the general direction of the lines slant downward; the whole handwriting is marked by weakness, tiredness, lassitude. For instance, t's remain uncrossed, loops are unfinished, the letters seem to be sluggishly inflated and slightly slanting.

Excitement, on the other hand, leads to increased liveliness because of greater muscular tension. The spatial extension and the pressure of the handwriting increase, the lines show an ascending direction, the rhythm of writing quickens. If this excitement is only a passing flare-up, these general symptoms may be considerable in extent and force, but even and constant. With the heightening of excitement the unevenness of the writing might become chaotic.

Frequently, irregular intervals in handwriting are also pathological symptoms; they show a considerable reduction in mental application, a natural corollary of a state of exhaustion or weakness. Such lack of continuity is often seen in the upper or lower strokes of letters. The sudden relaxation in muscular tension is caused by the abrupt weakening of the organism.

A handwriting in which the balance of the position and direction of the letters is disturbed because of the asymmetry of the lines has been called 'atactic' by Erlenmeyer. Those who show such signs have lost the ability to form their letters according to their will; their hands no longer obey them and they recede to the primitive, infantile beginner's status. To a slight extent the same disorder can be observed if something has been written with a stiffened, cold hand; to a larger extent, if someone suffers from writer's cramp. But it can also be a secondary symptom of weakness after a serious infection, of alcoholism, and of spinal trouble.

Trembling, shaking hands are unable to form straight lines. This can be frequently observed in old people, in hysterical persons, alcoholics and paralytics, and in those who suffer from nicotine poisoning and Bright's disease. There are otherwise completely healthy people whose hands have been unsteady ever since childhood. They have frequently learned to overcome this weakness, sometimes by a considerable effort—but their handwriting, instead of the palsied, trembling effect, shows a weak, 'atactic' character.

Sufferers from respiratory diseases often have to rest while walking. They do the same thing in writing when, leaning the nib of the pen on the surface of the paper, they take a brief, almost imperceptible rest. The small dot or line that marks such a pause is a definite clue to their illness.

A languid, sluggish handwriting parallels in retarded

people or those suffering from nervous diseases, their drawling, slow, hesitant speech. It is often apparent in the cases of nervous breakdowns or the early stages of general paresis.

At the other extreme, hysterical individuals, because of their temperament, might display all the pathological signs in writing. They all share one characteristic: the extreme changeability of their handwriting which means a complete lack of firmness, irregular spacing of lines, widely differing intervals between words and lines, an absence of direction and form. Such people usually employ the vaguely arched or looped forms, their lines often become confused, the word endings are mutilated, the starting lines are capricious and spiral to the left, which makes their writing chaotic and hard to read.

Agraphia (the inability to write or the loss of the ability) is caused by the pathological condition of a certain part of the cortex. The sick person is no longer able to express his thoughts graphically because the disease has stopped the co-operation of the cortex centres, and the possibility of writing movements and the association of optical and acoustic verbal forms have been lost.

Apart from the important medical applications of graphology—which we had to explore briefly before coming to our immediate subject—it also has a social significance in protecting society from crooks and criminals. Modern science has rejected the theory of Lombroso about hereditary criminals, and graphology does not accept such 'marks of Cain'. But there are certain physical and psychological qualities—such as weakness of the will, heightened sensuality, laziness, inclination to cruelty—which provide a fertile soil for criminals; though the crime itself is more often than not provoked by the milieu and the opportunity.

Scientific graphology cannot consider that its task is to

foretell from someone's handwriting whether he is likely to become a forger, a murderer or end as a suicide. Instead, it contents itself with establishing whether the 'subject' has such inclinations, whether he would be capable of such actions. A lack of sincerity, ruthlessness, spinelessness or dishonest thinking leave such deep traces in handwriting that the expert is able to identify them almost at first glance.

A lack of sincerity, a reluctance to show one's true colours, an excessive reserve, these are all shown in the *forms* of writing. O. Kellner analysed the handwriting of 40 habitual criminals. Of these, 21 used the so-called 'arched' form; 6 the 'festoon' or 'garland'; 6 the 'thread-like'; 4 the 'junction stroke', and 3 the so-called 'calligraphic'. Ten of the specimens displayed a jerking tendency to the left, another 14 tried to mask their egotism, ruthlessness, envy and greed with calligraphic neatness but disclosed it by other, unfavourable graphic indications.

Excessively neat, regular 'beautiful' handwriting, calligraphic 'masks', are preferred by the cautious, hypocritical, clever tricksters; sometimes it is the very attractive regularity of the writing that wins them the confidence of their victims. But the graphologist knows from experience that those who stick to patterns excessively, have little individuality; the smoother and more calligraphic their handwriting, the weaker their character. When such a script shows the mixed use of Gothic and Latin letters, a fusion of the stems of the letters, a wavy pattern of the lines and the absence of some letters, or parts of letters, the apparent evenness and neatness can be interpreted in their true nature.

Liars, graphologists say, love to embellish their letters with curlicues and these, just like the spiral terminal lines, show vanity and egotism.

The completely closed shape of the curves of 'a', 'o' and

'g' is evidence of secretive, reserved characters; those who add strong loops, are pathologically reticent and uncommunicative. A small circle, as an accent on the 'u', the 'mingling' of the downward strokes of 'm', 'n' or 'u' are also the signs of the lack of sincerity.

Criminals who have insufficient self-control to hide their weaknesses—for instance, those inclined to violence or of a weak nervous system—display in their handwriting quite openly their faults of character. Such weakness and unreliability are shown in the absence of a constant rhythm, in vague graphic forms, in an uneven and changeable employment of all the characteristic lines, and in a slight pressure of pen or pencil.

These are general principles, and only a few sample indications of how graphology works. Let me quote here a full analysis of the handwriting of a habitual criminal, as set down by the Italian graphologist Italo Riccordi, who did not know whose writing he was examining.

> . . . This is the handwriting of a gravely neurotic man who forms his ideas in the most capricious manner. A restless, harassed, totally confused man with a persecution mania developed forcibly, under outside influences. This is shown by the extension of the endings of the individual words which, in less extreme form, indicate suspicion, reserve, introversion. In his writing the terminal lines are often thickened, resembling clubs as if he wanted to give his suspicions a special emphasis; sometimes there is an impression of despair, the savagery of a cornered animal. Throughout the sample there is one amazing feature—in spite of all the confused and hysterical character his style is not bad, his structure of sentences is effective and in no way pessimistic—it even appears that there is some faint measure of planning for the future, though, for the time being, it is garnished with only faint hopes.

There is some logic in his thinking, shown by the almost completely linked writing but this is modified by the direction of the lines and words which change capriciously, varying between the strong leaning to the right (signifying excessive sensitivity) and leaning to the left (representing a bleak withdrawal). This is caused by a psychological state which is scared, terrified yet defiant, combining a good deal of self-confidence with despair.

His energies are scattered, he is unable to concentrate his attention and willpower. His efforts are episodic and not rationally directed. The strong and determined fundamental lines (for instance in the letters t) occur only irregularly and rarely.

Where the final lines of the downwards slanting long letters merge into another letter, he creates capricious, eccentric forms. These are the excesses of a sense of justice which has been deeply hurt—or believes itself to have been hurt to the point of causing a traumatic shock. The lines crossing the double t's are visibly aggressive in their direction but they are deviating from the rigid, bellicose forms, become soft, lose strength and are lost in the wavy line of fear.

In the final paragraph of the letter there is a strong intent of revenge, a longing for retribution and persistence. There is also a projected optimism in the background. A swinging zeal, an attempt to act decisively is neglected by a breathless, anxious, helpless overriding element which has still got some hope but not very much conviction.

The character sketch proved to be remarkably accurate though it did not help the police authorities in their actual apprehension of the confidence man. In the final analysis it helped the crook *himself* who was shown it after his conviction. He was so much struck by the self-portrait which he had created in his own handwriting that after serving four years of a seven-year sentence he actually reformed.

Raphael Schermann

The man who more or less personified the achievements and character of a psychographologist—the unique combination of a handwriting expert and a clairvoyant—was a sturdy, broad-shouldered Austrian born in Cracow. His name was Raphael Schermann and I have written about his exploits in some earlier books,* but his achievements were so varied, his work with the police and with the judicial authorities so extensive, that a good deal about him still remains untold.

He possessed a fantastic intuition which he combined with a thorough knowledge of the scientific elements of the subject. His reputation was that of a miracle-worker; he was compared to wizards and magicians. Yet he never dabbled in mysticism or faith healing. All he did was to use handwriting for character analysis and provide often extremely valuable aid to the police in criminal cases. His actual profession was that of an insurance claim adjuster—but he spent much of his time in helping others, and his greatest ambition was to *prevent* crime—to stop somebody on the way to law-breaking if that were possible. If he had been present in the office of Dr B, I am sure that those two unfortunate bank messengers would not have died.

In an autobiographical sketch which he prepared for my father, Schermann related how he began to collect envelopes as a schoolboy while his contemporaries preferred coloured pencils, marbles, stamps, or butterflies. He compared the handwritings with the people to whom they belonged. One day at school he discovered that the script of a hunchback

* *My Occult Diary*, with Cornelius Tabori (1950); *Pioneers of the Unseen* (1972).

boy showed certain flourishes which he could not detect in the writing of any of his other schoolmates. He succeeded—though not without a good deal of trouble, and with a remarkable persistence for such a young boy—in getting samples of the writing of several hunchbacks, and found that they all had certain characteristics, identical with those shown by his misshapen classmate. When one of the boys slipped a piece of paper into the pocket of an unpopular master with the single word 'Ass' on it, it was young Raphael who was asked to identify the miscreant. This he did easily—but begged the master to forgive the boy lest he should be ostracised for 'snitching'. He found that lame people also shared certain traits in shaping their letters. He was barely twelve when he started an album, asking all his acquaintances and friends, children and adults, to write a few words in it so that he could find the parallels between their hand and their physical appearance. In the course of several years his memory of handwritings and of people developed to an extraordinary degree; he amassed an amazing wealth of data on which he could draw, more or less subconsciously. Still later, he began to study the psychological side of the problem, the physiognomy of handwriting. Gradually he realised that whatever a human-being experienced was somehow mirrored in his writing, leaving its mark like a seal impressing itself on wax. He found that the handwriting of many people could be read—at least by him—like the open book of their past and future. In the end he only had to look at a piece of writing to guess how the writer would look; or, the other way round, by looking at someone, he was able to reproduce his or her handwriting to an astonishing extent of fidelity.

Around 1905 Schermann spent some time in the United States. In New York Dr van Hagen, a distinguished graphologist, proposed to go into partnership with him—but

Schermann preferred to return to Cracow. In 1910 he settled in Vienna and began working for a large insurance company. At the same time he started to demonstrate, in private, his analytical, prophetic and 'reconstructive' powers. Gradually his reputation grew. He was not only consulted by the police but was appointed as an official handwriting expert by the Central Law Court of Vienna. However, this was only a small part of his work. Above all, he was deeply concerned with helping troubled, unhappy people—without any financial reward and, very often, quite anonymously. Yet, almost against his will, he became a celebrity. The number of his 'clients' increased to hundreds, even thousands. The newspapers began to publish reports about his results—which appeared to be uncannily exact.

But Schermann always resisted being turned into a legend or a Cagliostro-like character. He hated dramatic gestures and loud publicity. He dressed simply; he deliberately cultivated the appearance of an ordinary, commonplace merchant or civil servant. Only his eyes, slightly veiled, pensive and melancholy, and his unusually large head set him apart from run-of-the-mill humanity. Still, he did change to a striking extent whenever he took a piece of writing into his hand. He seemed to literally grow in stature. His very speech changed—he used language plastically, with striking yet apt similes—like a poet. He painted character sketches with a few, telling strokes; above all, one felt the deep compassion, the pervasive humanity in his approach.

During the early part of World War I Schermann served with distinction in the Austrian forces but was badly wounded and after a painful spell in hospital, was invalided out of the army. It was in 1916 that my father, Cornelius Tabori, met him for the first time and about ten years later I was also present in Vienna during some carefully designed tests conducted with him. Max Hayek, Schermann's biographer, was also one of the group that tested Schermann's abilities. From all this material, collected before, during, and after these investigations, I have chosen a few striking examples to demonstrate the psychographologist's abilities.

In the spring of 1916 a grisly discovery was made in a derelict house at Cinkota, a shabby suburb of Budapest, the Hungarian capital. Seven hermetically sealed tin cylinders or barrels were each found to contain a somewhat shrivelled but otherwise well-preserved nude female body. After some concentrated and hectic enquiries the police established the identity of the victims. All of them were domestic servants, all had been lured to their deaths by advertisements in which a 'gentleman of independent means' sought a 'life-partner'. Their savings wheedled out of them, their few pitiful possessions pawned, they ended their lives in the cellar of a plumber's workshop. The only clue to the murderer was a postcard which he wrote to one of his intended victims—a few hasty lines which the Budapest police, totally baffled by now, submitted to Schermann.

The psychographologist was particularly excited by this specimen and provided a long analysis. Among other details, he declared that the murderer received the first impulse for his crimes from his frequent visits to prostitutes.

'It was clear to him,' Schermann continued, 'that his own humble position in life was insufficient to satisfy his passions and subconscious urges. He must have felt deeply unhappy, and even at a very young age he must have devoted much of his time and energies to his sex life. He needed variety and daily orgasms. Driven by his strong sensuality, he soon learned the art of seducing women of all types quickly and easily. I am sure that he must have been reading a good many crime stories—especially those dealing with the mass-killers of women. He must be a good-looking man with insinuating manners who had little trouble in striking up acquaintances; whenever he began a new affair, he tried to liquidate the earlier ones. It must have happened at this stage that he decided to get rid of a clinging insistent female by killing her. He found it unexpectedly easy to carry out his plan, no one suspected him, the woman's disappearance remained unnoticed—after which he was determined to use the same methods with any female who threatened to become a burden. He must have got rid of his own wife in the same way—of whom, I understand, no trace has ever been found since the entry at the registry office. He left his employment and set up on his own but his craft—whatever it was—was intended only as a cover, a front that enabled him to follow his murderous activities with greater convenience and security . . .'

Schermann was certain that the Hungarian Bluebeard acted alone, that he had no accomplices, although he might have involved others to strengthen his cover. '. . . His handwriting shows great self-control and even self-censorship; he is always on his guard and has never revealed his true self, except perhaps in the final moments before he finished off his victims. This self-control and self-censorship had become such an ingrained habit that he used it even in the most insignificant details; it is shown in his habit of painstakingly crossing the t's and dotting the i's, correcting an incomplete letter even when such correction would be hardly necessary . . .'

The psychographologist pointed to certain rounded, cone-shaped letters which indicated the jovial, amiable front that the murderer put on to attract his victims. Some of the flourishes pointed to considerable acting talent; but his writing was a clear sign that his friendly, informal manner was only pretence.

'A terrible struggle continued within him permanently and in many places there is a strong decline, descent of the words. His total reserve is most rigorous; the letters a, g and d are completely closed, without the slightest opening on top. The way he crosses his t's shows that he is jealously guarding his privacy, admits only very few intimates to his home or workshop—or those whom he has chosen to destroy. It is quite possible that he lived near a cemetery or was in some relationship to a gravedigger . . . An extremely cunning man, he preferred older women because he assumed that they had more money, a longer time to save a nest-egg. His burning sensuality served to kindle a responsive flame in some middle-aged spinster or long-neglected widow. His courtship naturally flattered them. And while they did not give him the sexual pleasure he sought, he could always find that with other, younger, prettier females. It is an interesting fact that whenever he uses the letter z (the lower case one) it is always 'crippled'—especially in female names. I assume that he must have hurt or strained his right hand when he crammed the bodies into those tin barrels. Such a sprain can last quite a long time and as he could not get help in this grisly task, his condition must have grown steadily worse and he could only follow a certain rhythm in writing. Thus his method of disposing of his victims is mirrored in the letter z. If he happened to spend some time in hospital, it is probable that he exchanged his own name card with that of a dying man and thus wiped out his identity . . . he was a born imposter. His sexual appetite was insatiable. I think he was most stimulated by redheads. The way his curved lines merge into a hard, straight line shows a rock-hard resolution and energy . . . I believe he is still alive and uses a different script, imitating the handwriting of the person whose name he has taken. But there are certain characteristics of his handwriting which he is quite unable to disguise. If there is some other material available—some registration form or other document he had to fill out—he could still be traced. Unfortunately the immense publicity given to the case excludes the possibility of any trap being set successfully. Maybe he has left something behind in the hospital where I am sure he has spent some time. He is a murderer but not a pervert. His orientation is strictly heterosexual if on the border of satyriasis . . .'

The murderer of Cinkota, though identified as a plumber called Béla Kiss, was never caught. However, his circumstances, his character, his activities were all fully established—and they fitted Schermann's description perfectly. Kiss had been called up immediately upon the outbreak of the 1914–18 war and was taken prisoner in the initial Russian offensive that invaded, though only temporarily, the land south of the Carpathians. For many years there were rumours of Kiss serving in the Foreign Legion, heading an important section of the Communist secret police—but nothing was ever established definitely. The chances are that he died in a prisoner-of-war camp, having taken a different name.

But Schermann's clairvoyant deductions were fully justified by the statements of those who had known Kiss and by two or three of his would-be victims who had escaped their doom by some accident or miracle.

Schermann's working methods were highly idiosyncratic—and effective. If he was handed a specimen, he looked at it for seconds, perhaps minutes. He did not read it—but appeared to absorb its character. His look was concentrated, intense, the corners of his lips quivered and even his cheeks began to twitch—as if expressing a most exhausting and demanding mental effort. It appeared that he was first trying to visualise the outline of the writer, his general image, the *leitmotiv* of his being. And then, usually after an introductory, decisive statement, he began a description which elucidated a whole range of new characteristics of the person involved. Max Hayek compared this to the drawing of water from a well. When he looked at a handwriting, Schermann could also be compared to a musician with a score in front of him, hearing a whole symphony, the voices of the instruments—but also recognising the shortcomings of the movements, the faults of the orchestration, the disharmonies and discords.

People who watched him—and I did myself on several occasions—often felt a cold shiver; amazement mingled with shock. His subjects were made aware of themselves with a suddenness and intensity which had something frightening about it. A stranger had become unwittingly familiar with their innermost secrets, sorrows, vices. They could hardly believe that a single line, even a word, or their signature was so eloquent, spoke so clearly to this interpreter. The handwriting became an alter-ego which experienced and suffered all that its author had experienced and suffered.

In December 1919 he was shown part of a letter with the signature carefully hidden. It had been written by a man who, three years previously, had been a prisoner-of-war in Russia. Schermann stared at it for about three or four minutes then dictated the following analysis:

> Born of a poor, simple family. Brooded a long time as to what career to follow, what road to choose. Did not find the right one. Became involved in some community from which he could not free himself. His life was bitter, he had little pleasure during the years. When he saw others, less talented, succeeding better than he did, he

> became embittered and this bitterness developed gradually into a universal hate of mankind. His parents and relatives noticed this and tried to steer him into a different direction—but all in vain. Slowly he sank deeper and deeper and was no longer master of his decisions. He mixed with a clique; his main concern was not to be considered weak. He was completely submerged by the influence of this group, became one of its leaders and yet was afraid of it . . .

When Schermann reached this stage in his clairvoyant analysis, he was no longer looking at the handwriting. He stared into space and spoke as if in a trance:

> Capable of any inhuman, horrible action—but he is not the executor, he makes others perform it. He is the voice of those who surround him, yes, he is almost their medium. In his later years he is going to play an important though short-lived role. And this role will be closely connected with the characteristics I have described. This can become his doom. If he is lucky and manages to find good people, maybe he will do good—but he inclines more and more to those in whom baseness and cruelty predominate. In this setting the low instincts will awaken in him, too; he will be even more ruthless than the others. And when the beast awakens in him, he will commit the most outrageous acts. He clings greedily to life. He is not one of those who desire death. Therefore he will do everything to save his life. But finally he will die a violent death. He will either commit suicide or he will be killed. I am inclined to think that he will die by his own hand . . .

The handwriting was that of Tibor Szamuely, the 'Marat of the Hungarian Soviet Republic', leader of the Communist terrorists who tortured and murdered hundreds of innocent people. In August 1919 when the Béla Kun regime fell, he was the only one among its leaders refused political asylum by neighbouring Austria—whereupon he committed suicide.

Violence, whether directed against oneself or somebody else, was always clearly discernible for Schermann. A woman who had murdered several children, betrayed both her actions and her pathological hate of infants in her writing. Some letters showed duplication—the image was that of a carriage with the brakes suddenly applied; the wheels were still performing a few revolutions before they stopped. A strange flourish above the letter 't' showed the rope with which the woman strangled her victims. In the middle of the loop there was an elliptical shape—symbolising the head of the child.

On the other hand, when a man disappeared and left a letter announcing that he was going to kill himself, Schermann had no difficulty in establishing his real intentions. He had committed a large-scale robbery and his purpose was simply to escape with the loot and start a new life of leisure. A small 'i' in his handwriting established two points—the double life of the criminal as someone shamming death yet actually alive. He had also put on, Schermann said, a huge false moustache on the model of the Kaiser's famous *es ist erreicht* (it is achieved) type. The halfconscious gesture with which he kept twirling this moustache was clearly mirrored in his writing. In two words (*wohl*—well and *ewig*—ever) this double feature of moustache and twirling were reproduced strikingly. One of the 'i's' had a double dot which expressed the uneasiness and his subconscious need to assure himself that he *did* still have his hirsute disguise. The loops of the letters 'o' and 'g' which were open at the bottom symbolised the shape of a hand reaching into a money-box. On the basis of these clairvoyant details the man was tracked down—wearing exactly the type of moustache that Schermann had described.

A few days later a woman called on Schermann and showed him a sample of writing. Schermann told her immediately that it was her own and that she was considering suicide. She denied it. Schermann insisted and told her that she carried a gun in her handbag, demanding that she should open it. She obeyed—and a revolver was seen. Schermann warned her not to make the attempt. For one thing, he said, she was too nervous, too distressed to kill herself—all she would achieve would be to cripple herself for life. This warning alone would be sufficient to inhibit her. Her signature—'Marie'—showed clearly the shape of a gun as soon as the handwriting was turned upside down. A few months later these flourishes disappeared from the woman's signature; she found her way back to sanity and life.

A Prague family was constantly plagued and hoaxed by anonymous telephone calls. For instance, Count B, an old friend of the house, left a message that he would visit them in the evening. The family made elaborate preparations, other guests were invited—but the Count did not put in an appearance. Later he declared that he had not sent any message and had actually been out of town. On another occasion the Baroness C invited the family to her box at the opera. They duly arrived for the performance—only to find that the lady had already disposed of the places in her box and knew nothing of the invitation. Schermann, asked to help, provided himself with samples of the handwriting of the family's various friends, both male and female. One of them clearly showed the outline of a telephone receiver. The hoaxer—a bitter, resentful old maid—was trapped and the nuisance ceased.

One of the most fantastic talents of Raphael Schermann was what he called 'reconstruction'. He was able to 'reconstruct' a man's handwriting after a single meeting—without ever having seen an actual sample—or, even more extraordinary, from a photograph of the person. Several striking examples of this strange ability were reproduced in Max Hayek's book. Admiral E. H. Seymour, Lord Jellicoe, the Austrian writer Dr Rudolf Lothar, the famous playwright Arthur Schnitzler, were some of his 'subjects'. And while Schermann's 'reconstructions' were by no means complete duplications of the original handwriting, the *basic characteristics* were always present, reproduced with uncanny fidelity.

All this would have been little more than an interesting series of experiments, a playful proof of Schermann's clairvoyant talents, but for the fact that he was also able to turn it to practical account. One of his most interesting cases was a burglary. He was asked by the insurance company for which he acted as consultant to investigate the matter. The police had found no clues—and yet large quantities had been stolen from one of the best-known Viennese department stores. Schermann sensed that some employee or other must be involved. He visited the place, inspected the staff discreetly, and his suspicions immediately centred on one of the assistants. He 'saw' the man's handwriting, 'reconstructing' it in his mind. Then he told the owner of the store to ask the young man to write a few words. The proprietor called his employee into his office. The young man only put two words on paper: '*I have . . .*' when Schermann, watching him, became convinced *that this was the guilty man and that he would confess his crime.* He signalled to the head of the firm who declared immediately: 'You are the thief!'

The young man jumped to his feet, protested violently, threatened to sue his accusers for slander and rushed towards the door. Schermann barred his way. 'You'd better stay. I know you're guilty—and your handwriting told me that you were ready to confess!'

The two men stared at each other. The shop assistant tried to defy Schermann's quiet searching look—but failed. Suddenly he collapsed, his resistance crumbling. He made a full confession.

'I see from your handwriting,' Schermann told him, 'that you're not completely depraved, that you can still be saved. You were corrupted by others, dragged into this ugly business. I'll put in a good word for you.'

The proprietor of the department store decided not to prosecute. The loss was made partly good, but *not* by the insurance company. The policy, as Schermann pointed out with a smile, excluded any thefts by the staff, so the owner had to be content, at least to some extent, with the confession and reform of a black sheep.

A similar though much more complicated case led to the prevention of a large-scale fraud.

As the years passed, Schermann was consulted more and more often by the police and helped them in various complicated criminal investigations. Sometimes he succeeded in cases where all police methods had been tried in vain; but in all these exploits of his he was only concerned with saving human lives from destruction. Anyone who had strayed from the path of legality, who was threatened by social or physical disaster, could count on his help.

On 28 June 1922, the Vienna Banking Union (Wiener Bankverein), one of the biggest banks of Central Europe, received the following letter:

Vienna
27 June 1922

To the Vienna Bankverein

I have pleasure to inform you that on June 23, 1922, Kr. 100,000,000—one hundred million crowns—have been placed to my credit at your bank; but as my drawing account is with the Anglobank, Vienna I., Strauchgasse,

I would ask you to transfer this sum after deduction of your costs, stamp duties and charges to my account:

Hermann Zagg, Anglobank, Central Branch

as soon as possible. As a fruit and vegetable wholesaler, I have considerable cash payments to make. My address is: Vienna VI, 8 Kapistrangasse IV.

Yours faithfully
Hermann Zagg

The letter was passed in the bank through the usual channels and reached the book-keeping department. There it was established that on 23 June 100,000,000 crowns had actually been deposited to the credit of Herr Hermann Zagg. There was nothing to prevent the transfer of this money to the Anglobank as requested.

But Herr Zagg was not to obtain this large sum (about £80,000 at the rate of the June 1922 exchange) so easily. Through the negligence of a junior clerk who had to deal with the matter, the transfer was slightly delayed. Herr Zagg's letter remained on this clerk's desk for a day or two and when he came to deal with it, it was necessary for him to check the credit balance once more.

The method by which such a payment was credited seemed to be fool-proof. At the teller's window the payment was entered in the so-called copy-book. The original of every page went to the book-keepers, the carbon copy remained in the teller's book. In this case the original page of 23 June showed Herr Zagg's hundred millions as the final item. But the junior clerk, wanting to avoid the necessity of asking for the original (which would have led to the discovery of his negligence and the delay caused by it), consulted the *carbon* copy. To his considerable surprise he found no credit entered for Herr Zagg. Of course, he could not keep this information to himself. When the original ledger was consulted, it was established that someone in the book-keeping department had entered the hundred millions as Herr Zagg's credit balance; someone who obviously intended to profit by the forgery. But no such entry could be made on the carbon copy as the ledger remained with the teller.

Suspicion for the false entry first fell on a young female book-keeper as the writing seemed to be hers. However, it was soon established that the script was merely a clever imitation designed to incriminate her and cloak the identity of the real culprit. A clerk dispatched to the address which the mysterious Zagg had given found that no one of the name lived there. It was now evident that the would-be swindler must have had an accomplice within the bank; someone who had made the false entry and was in a position to remove any letters or notices that would have unmasked the intended trickery.

The police investigation was unsuccessful and Schermann was called in. His first task was to analyse the original, handwritten letter of Herr 'Zagg'. Schermann declared: 'This is the writing of a fat, very tall man. He has a sedentary occupation which demands great concentration and leads to eye-strain. He probably spends a good deal of time bending over his desk. It is not mental work but one involving precision and accuracy. He may be a watchmaker or a goldsmith.'

This appeared to point to the fact that the writer of the letter did not work inside the bank. But the book-keeping entries must have been made by an employee. More than fifty of the bank clerks had their handwritings carefully analysed. Of one of them—it belonged to a man called LB—Schermann said: 'This is the man who made the entries. He is an artist of handwriting who can imitate the script of others with amazing fidelity. In this case he copied the writing of your girl book-keeper with complete success.

He studied her writing for a long time. He is a dedicated criminal. He thought up the whole scheme himself and then looked for an outside accomplice who was to write the letter signed by "Zagg". I see how he tried to persuade him to write the letter. I believe his accomplice is a goldsmith whom he dazzled with promises to provide him with much gold for his work. I know that it will be very difficult to make him confess though he knows by now that his trickery has been discovered. Give me another specimen of his handwriting—make him write a few lines *today*.'

This was done and Schermann, looking at the new sample, added: 'He already knows that he is going to be unmasked. He told his parents yesterday that he had planned and executed the crime—and asked them to forgive him if he got into trouble. His father and mother are ill. The mother declared that if her son were sent to prison, she would commit suicide. The father would also be unlikely to survive the disgrace. In spite of this, the son has no intention of confessing; he will insist on his innocence up to the very last moment. He is a scoundrel with a vicious character. Yet—for his parents' sake you ought to let him go. If you promise that, should he confess, you won't go to the police, I'll get him to admit his guilt.'

As the bank had not actually lost any money, the promise was given—after some hesitation. Schermann called the young clerk into his office. Everything happened as the psychographologist had predicted. The young man firmly denied his guilt. When Schermann asked him to write a few lines, he produced this:

Wiener Bank Verein
Organisations-Bureau
I had nothing to do with the hundred million crowns.
Vienna
11 July 1922

These few lines betrayed his plans. Though his Christian name was *Ludwig*, he started his signature with 'Loui(s)', crossing out hastily this French form of the same name and replacing it with the German one. Schermann thereupon told him that he had an accomplice who was a watchmaker and goldsmith and that he had discussed with him the plan to escape to Paris and live there under an assumed French name—Louis, instead of Ludwig.

This completely disconcerted the would-be swindler. He gave the name of his accomplice, who indeed turned out to be a goldsmith, weighing 18 stone! Not only his profession but his physical appearance had been correctly described by Schermann. The young clerk also spoke about his family and related the talk he had had on the previous day with his ailing parents, who had begged him to confess everything as they could not survive the disgrace of his arrest. This conversation, which Schermann had earlier put down on paper, was almost identical in every word with the young man's confession.

As the bank had escaped any loss, the young man was dismissed but no charges were brought against him. Later he wrote to Schermann:

> . . . I am sending you these lines to give you my solemn promise and word of honour to behave in the future at all times correctly and honestly. I want to express my deepest thanks for saving me and guiding me on to the right path after my first attempt at crime. God bless you for what you have done for me and my family.
>
> In eternal gratitude,
>
> L.B.

Among the many psychologists and scientists who experimented with Schermann, Dr Oskar Fischer, a professor of psychology at Prague University, was one of the first. He gave a fair and enthusiastic summary of the psychographologist's extraordinary gifts: 'The first important fact about Schermann's work is that it embraces both graphology and what we call telepathy. Even his graphological achievements, however, go far beyond the known limits of this science. He does not study the samples closely; a brief glance at the specimen is sufficient for him—and sometimes he prefers to turn the handwriting upside down. As a long series of tests has shown, he is also able to describe the writer's current mood; he can even establish, if necessary, whether he (or she) is hungry or well-fed. I repeatedly found that a few simple lines were sufficient for him to deliver a stirking character-sketch of the writer. He is also able to do this when his eyes are bandaged and he can only use his sense of touch to trace the writing. He had equal success when samples were given to him in sealed envelopes. After touching the envelope he was able to reproduce—or, if you like, reconstruct—the unseen handwriting with often amazing fidelity. The experiments also covered telepathic tests. Several people, including myself, evoked in their minds a certain person in Schermann's presence. Schermann was able to describe these persons, often providing a fantastically faithful character sketch and was also able to imitate their handwriting, again with amazing closeness to the original. The circumstance that Schermann gave graphological analyses while looking at the samples, that he was able to do this by just touching the sealed sample or the visible sample with bandaged eyes, his talent of "reconstructing" someone's handwriting—all this was examined and checked systematically. While Schermann's character analyses were so striking that I was convinced about the impossibility of any coincidence or accident, it must be admitted that his character and personality descriptions (at least for those not intimately acquainted with the subjects) did not provide a sufficiently objective series of proof of an outstanding or extra-sensory talent. If Schermann's gift was based on a regular physiological function, it was necessary to establish that his descriptions and imitations or reconstructions should be identical whether he was simply looking at the handwriting, touching it while his eyes were bandaged or producing his analyses through the experimenter's invocation of the same person purely in his mind. In order, therefore, to discover whether the three different methods produced a coherent, complementary method, I used a whole series of people whom I knew well, who had a clearly marked character, well-differentiated. Both the character analysis which Schermann produced and the "reconstruction" of the various handwritings were in every way correct—sometimes the originals were imitated with almost photographic fidelity. The series of experiments involved about 200 different cases. Out of these over 71 per cent were absolutely correct; about 8 per cent proved failures and the remaining 21 per cent could be described as indecisive. This statistical ratio established the regular, systematic nature of Schermann's talent and exclude all possibility of conscious or unconscious fraud . . .'

In a Vienna lecture a couple of years later Professor Fischer spoke at some length about what he called 'psychic transference'—the term with which he described Schermann's extraordinary gifts. Other specialists also conducted experiments with him—including the Viennese professor Moritz Benedikt, the Zurich physician Dr Paul Cattani and the Vienna psychoanalyst Dr Wilhelm Stekel. Their opinions completely agreed with the views of Professor Fischer.

Other psychographologists

Raphael Schermann was unique and he had no disciples or heirs. But in the last thirty years there have been a few, a very few people who have used handwriting as a basis of 'triggering off' their clairvoyance and did so while helping the police or the course of justice.

One of these was a Hungarian called Michael F. Fischl, a civil engineer who had studied graphology for several years and then discovered that he could draw conclusions and 'see' characteristics that had little or nothing to do with the script itself. His theory, which he developed after many false starts, was that a fragment, a minute portion of a person's ego, became transferred into his or her handwriting and that somebody sufficiently sensitive could 'read' it.

Fischl died young but he had two extraordinary successes during his brief life. One involved a friend of his, owner of a provincial printing works that was famous for publishing limited editions of great distinction. One day Mr K, the owner of the firm, showed Fischl a letter from a man who had applied for a position in his enterprise and whose qualifications seemed to be very impressive.

'Shall I employ him?' Mr K asked.

'No,' the graphologist advised him. 'Certainly, there is something extremely ingratiating and attractive about him. He quickly wins people's confidence—almost as if he would catch them in a net or with a lassoo. But don't hire him; you will have very unpleasant experiences if you do and within a short time you will be only too glad to get rid of him—which will cost you a good deal of money.'

Mr K accepted this advice. But months later the applicant called again at the printing works, argued against the injustice of refusing him a job and begged the master-printer to reconsider the matter.

Mr K, strongly influenced by the personality of his visitor, still remembered Fischl's warning. But he decided to test the graphologist's gifts—and hired the man.

Only a few weeks later he wrote to Fischl: 'It didn't take long for me to be convinced that your analysis of my new employee's character was in every way correct; I was more than wrong to doubt you. Within a short time he devised means to mislead and cheat me—and through his deceit and forgeries I have become liable for a very considerable sum which I have no chance to recover. I have, of course, notified the police but D has disappeared and I am told there is little chance of his being apprehended. What can I say? Perhaps I had to pay for my scepticism—but in a way it was well worth it, for I have learned my lesson . . .'

In February 1920 Fischl visited Zurich. At the time there was a sensational trial in progress involving a woman called Frau Buchmann who was accused of having poisoned her husband. The cantonal prosecution was led by Dr Brunner, the attorney-general of Zurich.

Dr Brunner was introduced to Fischl by a Zurich psychologist and invited him to his office where he told him about the case: 'It is now about eight weeks since Buchmann died. I received several anonymous letters accusing his wife of having poisoned him. I thought these serious enough to arrest her. But the investigation has produced absolutely no proof. Frau Buchmann denies everything stubbornly and declares that her malicious enemies have slandered her. Would you have a look at her handwriting?'

He produced a letter from his files and put it in front of Fischl. The graphologist examined it with close attention and then said: 'I see some shapes here which resemble the paragraph sign. That proves she has done something illegal. She is afraid of being imprisoned. I believe that she poisoned her husband eight or ten years ago . . .'

'That's impossible,' protested the state prosecutor. 'At that time she hadn't even married Buchmann. And Buchmann only died eight weeks ago.'

He looked at the date of the letter for the first time now—it was one which Frau Buchmann had written *three years* previously.

Dr Brunner suddenly had a small brainwave. He remembered now—Buchmann was the second husband of the woman under investigation. Her first one, a man named Hanhart, had died twelve years ago in a place called Steckborn. Was it possible that she had poisoned him, too?

Next day Fischl visited the police headquarters where Frau Buchmann was being held. A confrontation was arranged. She appeared accompanied by her two attorneys.

The state attorney introduced them and said then to the suspected woman: 'Mr Fischl will give us an expert opinion about your handwriting.'

The attorneys protested against calling in such an expert. They claimed that it was against the criminal code of the canton. And Frau Buchmann was also most reluctant to put pen to paper. But suddenly she seemed to change her mind. Defiantly, she sat down and wrote, without any hesitation or any noticeable excitement, two sentences which Dr Brunner dictated at Fischl's request.

Ich habe meinen Mann vergiftet (I have poisoned my husband)
Ich habe meinen Mann nicht vergiftet (I have not poisoned my husband)

Anna Buchmann

She was then taken away. Fischl examined the handwriting and declared: 'If Frau Buchmann did commit the murder, it was under an irresistible pressure. She had yielded to some outside influence and acted in a half-dazed state of mind.' And he added: 'She is going to *confess*.'

The prosecutor informed Frau Buchmann about Fischl's opinion. She laughed and declared, as before, that she knew nothing about any crime. Dr Brunner tried for two and a half hours to extract a confession from her—in vain.

As they were descending the staircase at police headquarters, one of the counsels for the defence said to Fischl: 'Mr Fischl, had I had prior knowledge of your expert opinion, I would never have opposed the analysis. You said Anna Buchmann had acted under an irresistible pressure. Even if I do not believe that my client is a murderess, if by some remote chance she is going to confess, I wish to use your statement as a mitigating circumstance . . .'

The confrontation took place on 20 February. On 26 February Fischl sent a written report to Dr Brunner about the handwriting of Frau Anna Buchmann. He explained his views and declared that she *had* committed the murder, in a mood of extraordinary excitement, inspired by a lust for revenge. She was a person who would be greatly impressed by the cross-fire of an energetic questioning and who could, in the end, be made to confess.

On 27 February Fischl, who had in the meantime gone to Basle, received a telegram: 'Murderess confessed!'

On Friday 5 March Frau Buchmann asked to see the public prosecutor again. She wanted to add to her confession—and admitted that she had poisoned her first husband, Hanhart, in Steckborn, twelve years earlier.

Fischl, just like Schermann, possessed the 'insight into the essential being' of men and women. Both of them saw in a handwriting something that could not be seen by the average handwriting expert. For instance, in Anna Buchmann's writing Fischl saw in the final stroke of the 'i' in the word 'poisoned' (*vergiftet*) a line that thrust to the right—representing a gesture of someone holding a dagger in his hand and prepared to strike with it. There was a recurrent element in the letter 'm' (which occurred three times in the German original) that showed an easily awakened passion for revenge if the writer was excited or provoked.

By dictating the two sentences, Fischl placed Anna Buchmann on an imaginary tightrope from which the slightest psychological shock could topple her into a confession. The first sentence was written straight and direct on the line of the ruled paper—her resistance was still strong—but by the second she had lost her balance, the sentence was dangling unevenly. Even so, she quickly recovered her self-control for the signature was once again in a straight line. Yet the momentary lapse was enough to provide a clue for Fischl's sharp eyes.

In another Swiss city Fischl was visited by a woman who told him that she was interested in graphology. She did not want an analysis—just some information. Fischl looked at her—and was able to visualise her handwriting, building it up from her physical appearance in his mind. What her writing told him was both tragic and unequivocal: she was on the verge of madness. He told her quietly: 'You didn't come to see me because you're interested in graphology. You've had a shattering experience, something that gives you no peace . . . that's why you visited me.'

'I don't know what you're talking about,' she replied with apparent calmness.

Fischl handed her a pencil and dictated the following sentence: 'Two months ago there was a great crisis in my life.'

Then he asked her to add her signature.

As soon as she had finished, Fischl cast a single glance

at the result and then said: 'You are a double murderess. You deliberately caused your child to be born prematurely—and when you found that it was still alive, you killed it.'

The woman protested angrily. 'You're totally mistaken!'

'Please don't get excited—I'll tell you in a moment when it happened.' And quickly, to deny her even a moment of reflection, he added a deliberate mistake: 'Four months ago!'

'No, only two!' she cried, unable to control herself. Then, realising that she had given herself away, she fainted.

Fischl chafed her hands, threw some water into her face. She recovered—and was now ready to make a confession.

Yes, she said, she had borne a premature child; she wrapped the little creature into a tablecloth and hid it in the attic. When next day she was alone, she went to fetch it—and found that its tiny hands and feet were still moving. She took it down to her rooms, locked the doors and windows, started a fire in the stove and burnt it until only the ashes remained.

Fischl realised how close to a total mental breakdown she was. He consoled her to the best of his ability, telling her: 'If you devote your life in the future to charity and good works, if you help others, God will forgive you!' He advised her to have a second child because if she gave it all her love she would no longer hear the accusing crackling which persisted in her ears whenever she saw the stove; she would no longer be haunted by the screams of the child she had burned alive.

In April 1920 when Fischl visited the Swiss town again, the same woman called on him once more. His simple, humane advice brought her peace. She was pregnant and she awaited her child with joyful acceptance.

Fischl's career was comparatively short and he had no official position with the police as his much more famous colleague had in Vienna. Yet he also had an impressive record and his early death was a considerable loss for psychographology.

Luce Vidi, a French clairvoyant, has specialised in a different kind of interpretation which is a combination of graphology and psychology through the special application of *ink-blot*. As we know, Rohrschach tests are widely used in psychology and psychiatry to establish the factors that go to make up the personality as a whole. Devised by Dr Herman Rohrschach in his *Psychodiagnostik* (Berne, 1923) they consist of getting the patient to say all that comes into his mind when he is presented with a standard series of patterns, some of them partly coloured, produced more or less at random by folding an ink-blot symmetrically upon itself. Psychiatrists have accepted it as a most successful test—or more accurately, probe—into the totality of human personality. The interpretation of the significance of the associations produced by the patient, when coded and classified, is fundamentally and primarily an intuitive matter. While it is true that the interpretations are standardised to some extent, they depend very greatly on individual experience and intuitive skill.

The Rohrschach tests have also been used as a differential diagnostic method when organic brain disease or damage is suspected—as well as between different psychiatric syndromes. A 'Rohrschach Exchange', a central bureau of somewhat esoteric information about the method, has been organised.

Madame Vidi has added some fancy embellishments to the Rohrschach blots. She claims that she has actually preceded the eminent psychiatrist by some years. She says that it was before the end of the 1914 war that she dined with some friends and told them: 'Last night I dreamt that I had made thirteen ink-blots on a sheet of paper, folded it into two and pressed it between my fingers to make the ink run out. When I opened the doubled sheet, I found a design—that of a wounded eagle.'

Madame Vidi interpreted this as a symbol of the defeat of the imperial eagle of Germany—and she was certainly right though she couldn't explain why such an important event should be revealed through thirteen ink-blots. But when she told of her dream at the dinner table, her fellow-guests urged her to try the same procedure in actual fact. She did so—and this time the result was a sword planted in the ground. This, too, she explained as another indication that the Kaiser was doomed.

On this rather slight basis, Luce Vidi has developed a lifelong career. For over forty years she has practised 'clairvoyant precognition' by inviting her clients to ask her a single question. Next she hands them a sheet of writing paper (for some reason its size had to be 27cm×21cm), marking the two edges 'top' and 'bottom'—for she finds that if the ink blot is 'read' upside down it never produces any satisfactory result. Then the person consulting her is asked to make thirteen ink-blots, the sheet is folded from the top to bottom, the ink is pressed down to give it a chance to form a pattern—after which all she has to do is to interpret the end product. Red ink is preferable to blue or black.

She has a whole file of these super-Rohrschach blots on display in her apartment not far from the Étoile in Paris. Her consulting room is literally papered with presscuttings, thank-you letters and reports of predictions and séances. She claims that she has been 70 per cent successful—which certainly excludes any accidental or coincidental element. I asked her whether she had any rational explanation for her method.

'Everything in the world is a symbol,' she replied. 'There

is a symbolism of faces, of hands, of handwriting, of the celestial signs, of colours, numbers, sounds. And as the symbols all "speak", I told myself: "If the ink-blots project symbols, one should be able to read the future . . ." '

The rest she has invented and developed herself. Among the 'designs' which she identified for me in her collection of ink-blots there were mummies, coffins, eagles, urns, cornucopias, cupolas, birds, houses, horses, crocodiles, devils and while I admit that some were reasonably recognisable, others needed more than a robust imagination to accept or discern.

Still, Madame Vidi quoted chapter and verse for her achievements. She apparently produced a 'symbolic silhouette' of Rasputin for Prince Félix Yussupov who, with some friends, killed the powerful Russian monk—and told the prince that he had no hope of recovering his estates. She told Madame de Saint-Exupéry that her husband was safe when he disappeared in a flight over the Sahara. (She didn't tell her that eight years later his luck would run out and he would be killed.) She forecast the marriage of a young Yugoslav princess—and Marina did become the Duchess of Kent. She warned Edith Piaf against burning the candle at both ends—although in vain.

She told me two incidents, both of them involving crime—one planned, the other executed. The first was a woman who came to see her one morning in great distress. The question she posed was certainly a startling one: 'Can you, please, tell me about a poison that leaves no traces? I have a husband who is a gambler, a drunkard and who beats me . . . I cannot bear it any longer—I must get rid of him . . .'

Shocked, Madame Vidi said: 'No, Madame, there is no poison that doesn't leave some traces . . . And there are other ways of solving your problem.'

She wrestled with her visitor's bitter resolution for a whole day—and in the end persuaded her to give up her plan. Instead, she got herself a job in which she soon rose to an executive position—and was able to divorce her husband, and even move to another city where she was safe from his unwelcome attentions.

The other police problem which Madame Vidi solved with her 'magic ink-blots' concerned a kidnapping. The police were completely frustrated because no ransom note, no communication whatsoever was received when the wife of a prominent Roubaix industrialist disappeared. The marriage was happy, the possibility of an accident or loss of memory was eliminated; and there were quite definite indications that the young woman was removed by force.

Madame Vidi gave precise instructions as to her whereabouts. She *had* been, indeed, kidnapped—by a Moroccan who was illiterate. He was trying to make up his mind how to find someone who would join him as an accomplice and who could write a ransom note—but couldn't decide whom to trust. He was found in exactly the spot that the clairvoyant had indicated—just in time to prevent him killing his captive in a fit of baffled rage.

It would be unjust to compare Schermann's and Fischl's forensic work with Madame Vidi and others who have used handwriting as the basis of attempting telepathic communication, forecasting the future or fulfilling other extrasensory and occult tasks. Ink-blots or the 'auras' of which some psychics speak in connection with handwriting are hardly applicable to criminal investigation. Yet the very rare psychographologists have rendered valuable assistance to the police, and if in recent years no one of outstanding talent in this field has appeared, it does not mean that their value and their achievements should be ignored or denied.

3
SECOND SIGHT

In the early sixties reports began to appear in the world press about some hush-hush experiments which were carried out under the auspices of the Pentagon. These involved telepathic communication between the nuclear submarine *Nautilus* and some spot in the United States—although the accounts varied as to whether it was New Mexico or Vermont. In any case, some of the articles claimed that important, even conclusive results had been obtained.

Not long afterwards news leaked out from the Soviet Union that systematic experiments in thought-transference were being conducted in Moscow and Leningrad. The rather disjointed information seemed to suggest (perhaps predictably) that the Soviet Government's interest too was primarily militaristic rather than psychical.

Then suddenly these experiments stopped. For it turned out that the accounts of the US project were nothing but complete fiction—invented by two French journalists and published initially in Paris whence it was picked up by other publications.

Such hoaxes, official and private, are not as rare as one

would think and this particular one had no public consequences; though it is a safe bet that whoever decided to initiate the telepathic research in the Soviet Union, found himself relegated to some minor job in Central Asia! But it shows the surviving and still vivid interest in the whole subject. Dr J. B. Rhine's work has now covered more than thirty years and though he has no longer any direct connection with the Parapsychology Laboratory at Duke University, North Carolina, it continues both in America and many other places. Parapsychology has become a subject of serious academic research in many universities. Dr S. G. Soal in Britain, Dr Ryzl in Prague, Professor Jule Eisenbud at the University of Denver have all tackled various aspects of extra-sensory perception.

We are not concerned here with all this painstaking work; some experiments went on for ten years and in the end petered out disappointingly. Nor is there much sense in entering into the details of the seemingly endless controversy that still rages between those who believe in the reality of telepathy and those who deny its existence on the basis that it has never been proved under conditions which *they* consider foolproof—nor can it be commanded or provoked at will. Quantitative evidence does not appear to be more convincing to us than even a single case in which coincidence can be excluded and in which someone has solved or prevented a crime purely by some mental process for which we have no materialistic explanation—at the moment. The men and women whose stories are told and examined here have actually achieved this; nor do they particularly care whether the sceptic believes them or not. The material has been taken from police archives or the personal memoirs of officials—most of whom are quite unconcerned with the pros and cons of psychical research, and who have simply registered the facts.

Spontaneous clairvoyance

On a snowy, winter evening on the Damrak, Stockholm, a young woman rushed into the headquarters of the ambulance service and demanded that an ambulance should be sent immediately to the Skansen, the famous outdoor folk museum, because her fiancé was about to commit suicide.

'But that's impossible,' the young doctor on duty told her. 'We can only answer a police call or an emergency. When did this happen?'

'It hasn't happened yet but you're going to be needed. I can see him preparing for death.'

Stammering, harassed, she told her own name and that she was the daughter of a well-known industrialist. She also provided her fiancé's name and address. He had been denounced for a serious case of peculation, but this was done by a band of blackmailers. The young man was a neurotic type, suffering from a mild case of agoraphobia, pathologically afraid of all publicity. He went out to the Skansen, wrote a farewell letter in one of the restaurants and left it . . .

The young doctor became sorry for the obviously distressed girl and offered to take her home. But on the way he had an idea.

'Wait a moment, I'll make a phone call . . .'

He rang the restaurant which the girl had named, and the headwaiter informed him that an excited, distraught young man had actually left a letter—addressed to his fiancée—and then rushed out, forgetting even his hat and coat.

This was convincing enough for the doctor to arrange for an ambulance. But, of course, he couldn't tell the driver where to go.

'I know!' cried the girl. 'Only—hurry—we might be too late . . . Not to Skansen . . . not any more . . . up to Lidingö . . . he's just behind the police station . . . I will direct you . . .'

As they crossed the bridge to the island, she cried out suddenly. She covered her eyes and whispered that the young man had fired his gun . . . and the bullet had struck him . . .

'But no . . . no . . . no he isn't dead. Let's hurry, please! Sound the siren!'

The ambulance rushed through the quiet villa quarters and when it reached the spot she had indicated, she jumped out and made straight for the snow-covered alley that ran at the bottom of some gardens. Ten minutes later they came upon the young man who had shot himself through the chest and was lying, unconscious, in a ditch. Luckily the bullet had missed the heart and had only lodged under his shoulder-blade.

A week later he could leave the hospital; and even before that, on the basis of the details which his fiancée and he supplied, the police had arrested the blackmailing gang. The girl who had performed this remarkable feat had never shown any sign of clairvoyance before—nor did she ever again use the gift which was apparently triggered off by her fiancé's peril.

Clairvoyance can be combined with precognition or can be restricted to a momentary, contemporary 'vision'. But in both cases there must be either some strong personal element involved—menace to someone beloved, a near relative or a close friend—or it must be deliberately provoked by demanding the psychic's active co-operation. Again, in both cases it can be extremely dangerous, psychologically and mentally, for the medium.

Count István Tisza, the Prime Minister of Hungary during the final years of the Habsburg Monarchy, was assassinated in October 1918. His assassins were never found although several people, accused of complicity, were tried and condemned.

The tragedy of the conservative and controversial politician (he was admired and hated in almost equal measure) seemed to be almost foreordained. Many of his supporters were worried about his safety; the day before he was killed, more than a dozen telephoned the leading newspaper, asking whether the rumours of his death were true. On the very afternoon of his murder a poster was exhibited outside the offices of the newspaper announcing the assassination, then removed when the news was denied—and then finally put up again when it was confirmed. Later it was conjectured that one of the planners of the assassination 'jumped the gun' and informed the paper even before the actual killers had carried out their murderous intentions.

Beyond all this somewhat vague theorising is a fact that Tisza's wife had clairvoyantly foreseen a previous attempt—and that it would be unsuccessful. On 29 October she had another strongly visual premonition and pleaded with her husband to leave Budapest; but Tisza insisted on staying put—and next day two rifle-shots ended his life.

No less than three telepathic incidents were recorded in connection with the tragedy. The strangest of them was that of an aristocratic lady who, more than 200 miles from the villa of the former premier, suffered the most extreme distress for several hours. Two of her close friends were present and to them she described various details which were only later established in the course of the long investigation. On the afternoon of the assassination she whispered in horror: 'Death is walking towards him . . . he is shot down . . .'

After a long and obviously painful pause, she screamed: 'Two bullets . . . here . . . oh, it hurts, it hurts!'

Her face twisted, her eyes rolling, she was clutching the same part of her chest where Tisza was hit by the fatal shots.

None of this, of course, could be admitted in evidence. But the two eyewitnesses of the murder—Tisza's wife and sister-in-law—confirmed it in every detail.

The telepathic projection of distress, of menace, has been recorded in hundreds of cases. One of them involved the eccentric and brilliant Belgian artist Félicien Rops.

Armand Herlot, a critic and art historian, knew Rops only slightly, hadn't seen him for years, and didn't think of him for months. But one day in December 1896 he felt some strange, urgent desire to visit him at once because he was in some serious trouble. He hurried to cross the town to the Chaussée de Waterloo near which Rops's isolated villa stood. He was within half-a-mile of the place when he felt clearly that Rops was on the point of death. This startled him the more because until then he hadn't heard of any illness or even passing ailment of the artist. When he arrived at the villa, he rang the bell but there was no answer. He knocked and beat on the door—nothing. Finally he managed to get into the darkened house through a back window and found Rops unconscious.

Seeking inspiration in 'the mortification of the flesh' whose appetites and passions he had pictured with such brilliance, Rops had fasted for a full forty-three days. He had lost almost 30lb (he had always been a spare, slim man) and had apparently reached the 'point of no return'. That morning, a few hours before his visitor arrived, he began to feel as if 'his body had separated from the senses' and had arrived at the 'final limits'. His grandfather clock had stopped one minute before noon and he had collapsed.

It took many weeks of careful nursing and a delicately balanced diet before the artist recovered his strength and was able to work again. Had Herlot not received the 'message' and acted promptly, he would have died. Of course, no one has been able to explain why, of all people in the Belgian capital, it was this rather casual acquaintance who became 'tuned in' at that particular moment to Rops's mind—or whether it was Rops who had unconsciously called for help or somebody else. The fact remains that this telepathic communication was established and saved a valuable life.

In recent years when thousands and even millions of men disappeared in prisoner-of-war and concentration camps, we have had many examples of a wife or a mother resolutely refusing to believe in the death of a husband or son. They 'feel' that he is alive—and sometimes this faith is rewarded with a happy ending, the long-lost prisoner returns. There are no global or even national statistics about the proportion of such cases, but the more striking ones often make headlines.

This happened to Frau Ludwig Lang whose husband was captured at Stalingrad. Years later she received two official notices that he had died. But she declared firmly: 'I don't believe it. There must be some mistake. He's alive.'

'How do you know?' asked one of her family friends who had become a suitor and was more than anxious to marry her.

'That's my business. I can see him—as clearly as I see you. He's travelling now—he's in great peril and suffers much hardship. Now I can see him surrounded by people who look Mongolian. He's escaping. Then—he's in prison . . .'

A third confirmation of Lang's death arrived but she still refused to believe it. On the contrary, she insisted that her husband was 'safe and well'.

Those who did not believe her, laughed at her, though only behind her back, for they felt it would have been cruel to try and shatter her faith. But when she began to tell her brother-in-law that she was in 'daily contact' with Ludwig, that she could even hear what he was saying though he was speaking in a foreign language which she could not even identify, the family sent for a psychiatrist. He treated her with great gentleness and consideration; in the end he asked her to put down on paper all she 'saw' or 'sensed' in connection with her husband.

This she did and gradually she stopped talking to others about her 'visions'. But there were other women who were in a similar position—indeed, in Frau Lang's own small Hessian town there were almost a hundred whose husbands had been posted 'missing'. They came to her for comfort. Sometimes she could help, sometimes the 'screen in her mind' was blank. She did not try to deceive; if she saw death or grievous suffering, she described it fully and honestly.

Five years after the first clairvoyant experience, Ludwig Lang came home—from Japan. He had escaped from the prisoner-of-war camp in central Asia and had made his way through Mongolia to China. Then, in the fullness of time, he managed to get to North Korea and thence to Japan. Out of seventeen episodes which his wife had put down on paper years earlier, fifteen proved to be right. He had become involved, innocently, in an ugly murder charge; he *had* been among Mongolians—he *had* come home. So did seven out of the ten prisoners-of-war whom Frau Lang had 'seen' alive.

Clairvoyant detection of crime

These are interesting and even impressive examples of what one might call 'spontaneous second sight', unexpected and inevitably non-systematic exercises of a psychic gift. Science will always feel uncomfortable about such cases because they do not fit into the universe of natural laws—that is, of *existing* or *explored* natural laws. The general rejection of anything that lies beyond and outside these has somewhat weakened in the last decades—or perhaps ever since Albert Einstein proved that the hitherto absolute was relative and opened the gates to the twenty-first century. But though less stubborn and less extreme, the rejection is still there—and it would be a hopeless task to convince the proponents of such views. This is not the purpose here. What follows is a limited gallery of clairvoyants who have actually worked with the police, who achieved success or suffered failure as all human beings do—but whose record was sufficiently impressive to raise a whole series of questions to which we, at least, have no answers.

The Frenchman W. de Kerler called himself a psycho-criminologist. A wealthy amateur, he was rather vain of his clairvoyant talents and liked to demonstrate them—although without any reward or any publicity. Later he became less reluctant to speak about his exploits but several of these have been recorded.

In January 1914 he spent the first week of the New Year on the Côte d'Azur. He paid a courtesy visit on the police prefect who was an old friend of Kerler's family. The police chief challenged him with a smile to find the burglar who had committed a highly profitable theft the night before. The police had not got far with their investigation, but the victim was the wife of a local bigwig with considerable political pull, and they were very anxious to recover the jewellery that had been stolen.

Kerler asked to be taken to the scene where he found a piece of broken glass—part of a window pane—with the impression of a palm. It was not complete but the greater part of the 'head-line' and a reasonable section of the 'life-line' and 'heart-line' were clearly visible. Kerler went into a self-induced trance and 'saw' a man of about 5ft 11in, with light-coloured eyes, prominent cheekbones, and a fair moustache and hair. He was a sturdy, muscular fellow and walked with a rolling gait, rather like a sailor.

Having given this fairly detailed description to the prefect, the latter produced his records from which three photographs were extracted and placed in front of Kerler for study. Without the slightest hesitation, he picked one of them.

A few hours later the suspect was found in one of the bars of La Napoule and brought to headquarters, where his palm-print was compared to the one found on the fragment of the window pane. They were identical and a confession followed promptly.

Two years later Kerler was again in Nice. Early in April the chief of the police of the Alpes Maritimes department telephoned him, asking for his help. There had been another burglary, this time with an even more valuable haul. And the criminals had left no fingerprints behind.

The burglary had taken place in a villa at Cannes, on the Boulevard d'Alsace, behind the railway yards. Here an eccentric rich rentier had settled during the war. One of his peculiarities was that he always kept a few hundred louis d'or, together with silver coins worth several thousand francs and some rings and bracelets, in a small, metal-lined cabinet. (He was very fond of jewellery himself and always wore several rings and gold chains.) Returning home at two o'clock in the morning he stumbled over the small cabinet in his study—it was empty. There were absolutely no clues; the burglars had entered by using a skeleton key and obviously had no difficulty in getting the portable safe open. After several days had passed without any success in the investigation, the police turned to the 'psychocriminologist'.

Kerler began by placing two chairs at a distance of about a yard from the small table on which the cabinet usually stood. He made the victim of the burglary sit down on the chair on the northern side while he took his place opposite. He deposited the portable safe—whose strong lock was also opened by a skeleton key—on his knees. Then he took both hands of the rentier between his own and induced a mild trance-like state in himself during which he did not lose his consciousness. The first result was a clairvoyant vision: a handwriting resembling a fly's legs; its ascending lines were thin but black and clearly marked while the descending ones were clumsy and thick. Kerler asked the owner of the villa whether he knew such a handwriting. Monsieur Marquette, the rich rentier, said yes, but he couldn't possibly believe that the person who wrote such a hand could be involved in the robbery; he was a close friend. Kerler paid no attention to this; he fixed his eyes on the empty cabinet. His vision became 'more complete'. He saw the face and figure of the man to whom the spidery handwriting belonged. He asked Monsieur Marquette to find letters, postcards, photographs of this man. Finally he asked some questions.

'How long have you known this person?'

'Two years.'

'When did you last see him?'

'Two months ago.'

'If he was such a close friend—why such a long interval? Did you have a quarrel?'

'Not a quarrel—we just found we couldn't agree on certain things . . .'

'What was his profession?'

'Really, Monsieur Kerler—what has all this got to do with your investigation? I think he was a deep-sea fisherman for a long time, then he became a cook, later worked as a waiter in a café . . .'

'He was a sturdy man, wasn't he? And rather aggressive?'

'You might say so—he certainly had a strong influence on his friends . . .'

'So he had many friends?'

'I think so. They were all of a lower class than myself . . .'

'Thank you, Monsieur Marquette. I think I'm on the right track now—and I'd better go back to the police chief's office.'

He took a sample of handwriting and a photograph of the former fisherman with him. Nor was it difficult to find the same photograph in the police archives. The man's record dated back three years. His first encounter with the police was in connection with a robbery where he was suspected as an accomplice. He belonged to a gang of rowdies who terrorised Marseilles and the coast. He had been banned from Cannes. His description was sent to the Marseilles police and within twenty-four hours he was arrested, together with one of his associates who was helping him to sell the stolen jewellery. They found the silver coins in their room, but he had already smuggled the gold pieces into Italy and sold them in Ventimiglia through a third accomplice. Monsieur Marquette—who, like many in the arrested criminal's circle, was a homosexual—was reluctant to prosecute but Vouland, the burglar and bully, was sent to prison for seven years for other crimes he had committed.

In October 1925 the German newspapers published long

accounts of a trial that was spread over several weeks. The accused was a teacher named August Drost who had a considerable reputation as a clairvoyant and who had succeeded in a number of cases where the police had given up or had been unable to produce quick results. The trial was not about the practice of second sight, but about the question of whether such power existed at all. The presiding judge at the Bernburg court, having listened to a whole procession of witnesses, remarked testily: 'If it cannot be proved here that the facts could have become known to the medium in some other way, then we are certainly faced with something extraordinary, I may even say, miraculous . . .'

Drost was accused of misleading people in order to 'obtain illegal financial advantages'. The court had to decide whether he had acted in bad faith—and whether he had, indeed, profited materially—illegally or not.

Not a single case was produced in which Drost had offered his services or forced his intervention on anybody. Only once had he called apparently uninvited, and that was on a distinguished doctor, a *sanitätsrat* in Ballenstedt, this being also one of the very few instances in which he had asked for a fee. He didn't get it. During the trial it turned out, however, that Drost made the journey to Ballenstedt at the request of the chief public prosecutor of Dessau, a Dr Birkner, who communicated through the Bernburg state attorney with Drost. 'Official channels' had been used. Strangely enough, the same people induced the quietly spoken, inoffensive teacher to use his psychic talents—and then arrested him and kept him five months in 'preliminary custody'.

Certainly, the Ballenstedt incident looked quite damning. Before he went into a self-induced hypnotic trance, he had been given details of the burglary he was supposed to solve. He had visited the house which had been robbed, but the séance produced nothing very helpful. No arrest of the guilty parties followed and Drost was unable to give any information about the whereabouts of the stolen goods. Yet something strange *did* happen: Drost declared that the thief had taken from the *sanitätsrat*'s desk a 'greenish book' —something 'with which one makes money'. When he was asked what he meant by this, he said: 'Something with which one collects money.' Thereupon the victim went to his desk and found that his cheque book was missing— something he hadn't known himself. Two police officials who were present confirmed this incident under oath.

Drost's trial raised the whole problem of the definition of clairvoyance. No one seemed to be able to offer a final, comprehensive one, but the experts more or less agreed that at least for the time being it would cover the 'cognition of a fact that was unknown to all present or at the most existed only in their subconscious'. In the Ballenstedt case there was no question of the subconscious—for the robbed doctor did not know about the cheque book—but of 'pure clairvoyance'.

Another case that was discussed at the trial concerned the wife of a factory-owner in Dingelstedt who had lost her valuable jewellery to a thief. She had certain suspicions and went to Bernburg to consult Drost. She did not give any details before the session. And Drost provided two names: one of them a girl who occasionally helped out in the household, and the other that of a Dingelstedt merchant who sold and bought articles of gold. He added: 'Child sick— poor boy . . .'

The two people named by Drost were questioned, but their guilt could not be established. However, the Bernburg teacher did not mention their names in order to accuse or throw suspicion upon them. The manufacturer's wife was amazed when she heard the names—for the medium had never known these, nor had she thought of them as responsible for the loss of the jewellery. But four months later the lady found the stolen articles in a drawer which she opened every day—and in which the clothes of her sick child were kept. After the jewellery was found, two more séances were held with Drost. During the first one he indicated that the property had been recovered (though of course no one had told him). During the second a policeman brought a locked casket along; he knew nothing about what it contained but Drost described the contents: one of the lost brooches and a memorial medal with a golden frame.

How the stolen things actually 'returned' could not be established. But Drost had quite undeniable successes. A watchmaker and jeweller called Schade lost a large sum of money and various other valuables in a burglary. One of his assistants called Walter was suspected at first but proved his innocence. Schade turned to Drost for help. At the same time a young girl called Louise Rennecke (Walter's fiancée) offered her aid. She, too, was a medium and had worked several times with Drost. They both participated in a séance during which a strange question-and-answer routine developed between them, a trance dialogue. In the course of this they both named a man called Franz as the thief. Then Drost added that the money and the valuables were hidden under a layer of straw in a house of the Grosse Wasserreihe in Bernburg. 'Franz', Miss Rennecke said, was married and had two children. The police soon discovered a man called Franz Müller who filled this description and the larger part of the stolen goods was found in the place indicated—thus clearing Walter.

One of the most dramatic cases in which Drost was involved concerned a murder and robbery in the house of a farmer named Rockmann in Calbe. In February 1923 someone broke into the farmhouse while Rockmann and his wife were away. The intruder was obviously surprised by a middle-aged farmhand called Schlosser—who was found brutally battered to death. There were no fingerprints or other clues but the farmer's savings which he kept inside a grandfather clock were stolen, together with a quantity of plate. Drost was called in and in his clairvoyant trance stated that *two* people were involved whose names were 'Edde' and 'Aefer'. No one could be found answering to these names and Drost was once again consulted. This time he gave the name 'Adam' whose home had been already searched though nothing had been found. Adam Jaffe, who lived in the small village near the Rockmann farm, was once again examined. This time he came up with two names—two itinerant workers who had questioned him about Rockmann's habits and wealth. Their names were 'Schäffer' and 'Ende'. A few days later they were both arrested in Hanover and confessed to the murder and robbery. Thus the clairvoyant 'read' the names—but phonetically rather than visually, which explained the discrepancy.

Drost was acquitted and continued to practise his unorthodox and unofficial detective work. He died in 1943, all but forgotten; the last ten years of his life were spent in discreet retirement for he was afraid of being exploited by the Gestapo, and while he did not belong to the sparse ranks of the anti-Hitler resistance, neither could he bring himself to aid the Nazi regime in the slightest measure.

In February 1925 a young woman named Amalia Leirer was found murdered in a Budapest apartment. The post-mortem established that she had been dead for over three weeks—but the corpse lay undetected behind closed doors though part of the large subdivided flat had been occupied by a well-known comedian and his family.

Amalia Leirer was a highly paid courtesan, the girl-friend of a Dutch businessman who visited her for a week or so every few months. He provided handsomely for her and she was several cuts above a common prostitute; for one thing, her father was a wealthy property dealer and she had chosen her profession mainly because she wanted to escape her constricting and old-fashioned family setting. She was also something of a nymphomaniac who needed sex in frequent and generous portions. Apart from her regular and generous patron she had a whole series of lovers, some of them chosen indiscriminately.

The murder which had sensational and bizarre features naturally occupied a good deal of space on the front pages. The police promised an early arrest but seemed to pursue the investigation with more than the usual ineptitude.

About a week after the discovery of the body a Budapest art dealer named Charles Schenk called at police headquarters with a striking and strange tale. He told the chief inspector in charge of the case that the previous evening when his wife was busy with her household chores, she suddenly felt that she was 'being possessed by spirits'. She had never been interested in the occult and knew almost nothing about spiritualism or trances. But now, driven to some irresistible urge, she sat down at the dining room table, having procured pencil and paper. The pencil began to move—a typical example of 'automatic writing'—and within an hour she had produced four closely written pages. Schenk claimed that the 'spirit' that had manifested itself through his wife was the ghost of the murdered Amalia Leirer.

In the alleged posthumous 'interview' the pretty blonde courtesan revealed that she had been killed by 'someone whom she loved' but who had treated her badly. She also provided an exact address for her murderer's whereabouts:

it was No 12 Templom (Church) Street in the Slovak city of Bratislava, called Pozsony by the Hungarians.

The police received this communication 'from the Beyond' with understandable scepticism—but the chief inspector immediately telephoned to the Bratislava police, asking them to establish whether there was such a street in the city; also, whether the young man named by the spirit communication lived there. The only immediate answer given was that a Church Street did exist.

Reporters called on Mrs Schenk, a plump, handsome lady with nothing eerie or particularly spiritual about her. She explained that on Saturday night, before her strange experience, the furniture had started to crackle and rattle in the dining room and she felt a chill. The only paper she could find was a copy-book of her schoolboy son's; the message was expressly intended for the police, which was why she sent her husband on Sunday morning to the headquarters of the investigation.

She produced for the journalists the actual writing. It was faint and written in obvious haste, with nervous, uneven letters. Mrs Schenk herself had some difficulty in deciphering it for the reporters: 'I am the girl who was murdered four weeks ago. The murderer was a boy whom I loved but who treated me badly . . .'

Mrs Schenk remarked at this point: 'When she said this, I stopped and asked her whether she was really telling the truth, for I had heard that there were ghosts who are just as malignant and deceitful as people are in the flesh. But the answer came quickly: 'God be my witness, I am telling the truth. I must tell it or I couldn't ever find any rest.'

She also disclosed that her murderer had taken away various valuables.

'The silver . . .', the automatic writing continued, 'is in the home of a relative of the killer . . . here in this city.

He comes from a better-class family but has sunk into the deepest mire. I had known him when he was still well-kept and good-looking . . . Send this to the police, please . . .'

Mrs Schenk asked at this point whether the murderer wasn't someone about whom rumours had been spreading in the capital. (At a certain stage in the investigations the police had hinted that Laurence Leirer, Amalia's father, was the Number One suspect.)

'No, no, all that rumour and gossip are wrong,' protested the 'spirit'. 'God has punished me because I was ungrateful and disobedient to him. But everybody has to suffer because ingratitude is a grave sin in God's eyes . . .'

'Where is the murderer now?' Mrs Schenk demanded.

'He is at home in Pozsony, at No 12 Templom Street . . . he is reading the newspapers and gloating, the wicked one! I came to you, by the way, because I know that you have read all the reports about my murder with close attention and so I knew you must be interested in it. Are you sorry for me?'

The newly created medium now wanted to know what was the *profession* of this young man in Bratislava. Amalia Leirer's spirit appeared to be quite willing to talk at some length.

'An unemployed waiter with whom I was on intimate terms and who knew my circumstances. I was afraid of him because he threatened to finish me off but I wouldn't believe that this would happen so quickly. He's brown-haired, smooth-shaven, he wore a grey suit, patent leather shoes, a fur-trimmed black overcoat, a soft hat with a bluish-grey band. He's about five foot nine, his face is rather long. And pay attention to what I am saying now: I called him Jule . . . my dear little Jule . . .'

When she got to this point, the medium asked her to write down her name. The answer was '*Rita Leirer* . . .'

Mrs Schenk expressed her scepticism.

'Don't doubt me,' the 'spirit' replied quickly. 'This is a great sin. I came to you because I saw that you were reading the reports and I knocked to warn you . . .'

The Bratislava police sent a more detailed report the following day. There was no one of that name or answering to the description the 'spirit' had supplied, at No 12 Templom Street.

About a week later the Budapest police and the firemen were jointly engaged in a complex rescue operation. A young man had climbed one of the tall pylons of one of the Danube bridges which was topped by a *turul*, a legendary, eagle-like bird of Magyar prehistory. There he proclaimed, loud and clear, that he was the murderer of Amalia Leirer. But he also declared that he was the Archangel Gabriel who had come to destroy the sinful world, and that anybody who touched him would be immediately burned to cinders.

The police and the firemen, however, risked this unpleasant end and managed to get him down. He was obviously mad and they put him in a straitjacket. After a short struggle he subsided and became quite meek. In the lunatic asylum of Lipótmező he gave his name as István Kovács (Kovács is the Hungarian for 'Smith' and there are thousands of people who are called this) and his profession as an electrician. He was such a model patient that after a few days the straitjacket was removed. Whereupon one evening he simply walked out of the place and disappeared.

Several months went by. Then one day a pawnbroker informed the police that a silver candlestick which may have been part of the Leirer loot had been offered to him for sale. This time the detectives bestirred themselves and before long arrested a middle-aged man called László Okolicsányi who had been involved in extreme right-wing terrorist acts. He admitted that a friend of his had left a quantity of silver and other articles with him. He knew him as Gyula (Julius) Pödör—an unemployed waiter who occasionally also did electrical repairs.

The chief inspector began to put two and two together—especially when Okolicsányi's description fitted the lunatic who had made such a public confession of his guilt. Somewhat reluctantly, he sent two detectives to Bratislava. There, at 12 Templom Street, they found 'Jule' Pödör. When he saw them approaching—he had a room on the top floor of a small tenement house—he shot himself.

No one thanked Mrs Schenk. But then, her clairvoyance had worked in a very peculiar way. She had looked both into the past and the future. And the police could have hardly acted on her tip—*which was not to become actual fact until several months later*. But the case is well documented. It also shook Mrs Schenk so much that she never again listened to any spirit messages—though, as she told me when I interviewed her several years later, it 'wasn't for any lack of opportunity'.

Douglas Hunt, in 1967, said of another Hungarian clairvoyant: '. . . it is no exaggeration to say that there are hundreds of people alive today who owe their lives to him.'

This is certainly an extraordinary tribute to a man whom very few people ever heard of outside his native Hungary.

One of his most celebrated exploits was reported in an exile paper, published in *Magyar* in the Argentine whose issue of 10 February 1953 carried the full story.

It began when a Hungarian refugee called Sándor Sebők disappeared from the Argentinian village of San Vicente. Sebők was something of an eccentric and a restless creature, always on the move. One of his latest schemes had been to try and breed angora rabbits—in his bathroom.

Two of his close friends suddenly received letters from him, asking them *not* to visit him. But the letters were so contradictory and confused that they did exactly the opposite and travelled to San Vicente. The modest house in which Sebők lived was locked. But they managed to get in through the open bathroom window—where they found themselves surrounded by hungry and emaciated rabbits. They searched the house but there was no trace of Sebők.

Further enquiries were made and it turned out that another Hungarian called Kandikó, who was a former owner of the house and who had now and then helped Sebők in his various, not very successful enterprises, had also vanished. The Argentinian police pursued the matter with moderate enthusiasm—but gave up fairly quickly. The two men had probably just shaken the dust of San Vicente from their feet and had either left the country (it was easy enough to slip from Buenos Aires across the river into Uruguay) or had their own very good reasons for keeping their whereabouts to themselves.

István Tahi, however, one of Sebők's two friends, suggested that János Kele should be consulted. His companion had never heard the name. Tahi explained that Kele had been working with the Budapest police for more than ten years. He was a clairvoyant with a phenomenal record of being able to trace missing people and suicides.

Tahi sent him one of Sebők's letters to see what Kele could 'make of it'.

Kele replied promptly enough. He declared that the letter had been written under 'evil pressure' and its writer subsequently murdered. He would be found buried some 2ft underground and about 100ft from the house.

He also added several landmarks and other details so that the police had no difficulty in finding the exact spot. The surface had been smoothed and stamped down and grass had been planted over it. There, exactly 2ft below the surface, they found Sebők's lifeless, mouldering body.

Nor did it take long before Kandikó was arrested in a small provincial town. He confessed that he had forced Sebők at the point of a gun to write the letters, and had then shot him. Having interred the corpse, he had departed with everything of value he could find in the house.

For the people involved in Argentina—more than 6,000 miles from where Kele was living—it was inexplicable, verging on the marvellous. For Kele it was all in a day's work—a work he had carried on for about twenty-five years.

A plump and short man who looked like any ordinary member of a crowd, Kele had one unusual feature: his eyes, which were large and had an expression of great compassion and understanding. He was like Will Rogers, who said that he had not found any member of the human race whom he really disliked.

Born in Hungary, he moved to Germany after World War I. He settled in Leipzig where, quite without design, almost automatically, he began to talk to strangers, telling them about their lives, their past, their problems. Before long he found himself besieged by people seeking advice and help—which he gave freely and without any reward.

He denied that he was a clairvoyant—though he obviously was one. 'I am only a good psychologist,' he declared. At the most he admitted that handwriting gave him the sort of clue which Raphael Schermann found in graphology. But when Professor Hans Driesch and other outstanding members of Leipzig University tested him, they classified him without the slightest hesitation as an 'extraordinary psychic', a 'classic clairvoyant'.

His fame spread and soon a number of journalists called on him—most of them with the avowed intention of unmasking him as a fraud. But the scoffers all left as converts—for Kele was able to tell them their innermost secrets with 100 per cent accuracy.

In 1930 a lady consulted him. Her son was about to have an operation for a brain tumour. Another son had already died after similar surgery.

Before he answered, Kele began to sweat profusely. Then he asked the lady whether she had any relatives or friends in the tropics. Yes, she replied, her husband was working there on a long-term assignment.

When was he last in Leipzig? Two months ago. Had he brought any gifts?

Yes, a native carpet.

At this point Kele interrupted the consultation and telephoned the hospital, asking the doctors to postpone the operation. At first they demurred but he invoked Professor Driesch's name and after that they were willing to listen to him.

'Send an entomological expert to the boy's home,' Kele told them, 'and have him examine thoroughly the carpet hanging on the wall above his bed.'

After some hesitation, the hospital authorities agreed to do as Kele demanded. Within a couple of hours they telephoned Kele: 'The carpet has been examined. We found a tropical insect in it. Its bite produces exactly the same symptoms the boy has—similar to those of a brain tumour. No operation will be necessary . . .'

When Hitler came to power, Kele—an 'Aryan' but an anti-fascist—returned to his native country. Within a few months Dr Stephen Szimon, a deputy police chief, organised a special police department concerned largely with tracing missing persons and would-be suicides. Some three years later Dr Szimon gave an interview to the *Daily Mail* in which he stated that Kele averaged 80 per cent accuracy.

'There are days when he is 100 per cent accurate,' the police chief added.

He was asked to give a concrete example.

'On 28 December 1935,' Dr Szimon recounted, 'a distracted woman informed us that her niece had run away, leaving a suicide note. We turned the case over to Kele who, after a short time, said that the girl had gone to the Elizabeth Bridge to throw herself into the Danube—but had changed her mind at the last moment. The police were warned that she might either take a train somewhere or throw herself under one. Special patrols were sent out and one of them soon found the girl and restored her to her aunt.'

But Kele's main concern was the rehabilitation of the mentally crippled and the desperate. He was more interested in helping those whom society had rejected or whose brains had become overshadowed by some tragedy or handicap than in the pursuit of criminals. But he did help the police in the solution of a number of criminal cases, including murder—though he always did this with some reluctance.

In 1946 Kele left Hungary, for he felt acutely uncomfortable under the Soviet occupation and the possibility of a total communist take-over—something he foresaw quite clearly some two years before it actually happened.

He moved to Germany and continued his work in the Federal Republic. During the last years of his life he conducted some experiments with Dr Carl Osis of Duke University where Professor Rhine had done his important ESP work. Dr Osis sent him samples of writing, and from these, paralleling and in some cases surpassing Schermann's work, he was able to give full details of the writers' temperament and situation. In many instances he was able to diagnose diseases.

When he died in 1957, he left no riches and his fame was

restricted to a comparatively small circle, for he sought no publicity and found in his striking achievements his highest reward.

A clairvoyant who did not depend on handwriting or any other physical contact and who sought neither reward nor celebrity, Nicholaas van Rensburg's precognitive genius was recorded officially in a Government Blue Book of the Union of South Africa—a unique acknowledgement of a seer's talents. On 26 February 1915 the report stated: 'He was a prophet not without honour in his own country. On many occasions he had given proof positive of the possession of extraordinary powers of prevision.'

All his fore-knowledge came to him in dreams—though these occurred often in self-induced or automatic trances.

Nicholaas van Rensburg, as F. Addington Symonds records, was born in 1862 in the Western Transvaal, the son of a struggling Dutch farmer. His 'second sight' manifested itself early enough. Once, when his father was away from the farm, the native servants began to show considerable hostility. Mevrouw van Rensburg became alarmed, collected her children and was about to abandon the farm. Young Nicholaas, not quite ten, told her at this point that he had a dream in which the Lord Himself assured him that none of the family would be harmed. The young boy was so self-assured and positive that he convinced his mother of the reality of his experience. They stayed. Before long the farmhands seemed to calm down, their sullen looks disappeared, their mutterings ceased—and the family was safe.

Of course, Mevrouw van Rensburg told her husband and others of the incident; other, similar or even more striking examples followed and before long young Nicholaas acquired a local reputation as a 'seer'. He did not enjoy it. He was shy and retiring by nature, intensely religious, and during the next few years he avoided even the sparse limelight the isolated community could have provided. He worked hard on the farm, helping his father who needed all the help he could get.

In 1899 came the Boer War. To many South Africans this was a crusade and Nicholaas joined Oom Kruger's army. He was sent to a camp in the Taungs district. The unit stationed there had just won a skirmish over the British; they were celebrating it gaily, singing psalms of thanksgiving, only van Rensburg took no part in the jubilant rejoicing. He was sitting apart from the others, sunk in a kind of private meditation, totally unaware of his surroundings. Then he suddenly jumped to his feet and cried: 'I have had a terrible vision! I have seen farm-houses . . . burning. I have seen women and children . . . taken away . . . driven into captivity.'

His comrades did not take him seriously and refused to believe his 'meanderings'. Whatever foolish dreams the young man had, could not be reality. But the 'seer' was so distressed and so insistent that his commanding officer, thinking he was suffering from some mental disturbance, sent him on sick leave.

He had left the camp only a few hours when news arrived. The conflict had spread and intensified, becoming ugly and cruel. In the fierce clashes many farmsteads were put to the flames; women and children who in most cases were the only ones left at home were removed to prison camps. Van Rensburg's prophetic dream was readily and sadly recalled now by his comrades and when he returned, he was received with deep respect. It was accepted that his visions were God-sent and must be taken seriously.

He now travelled from one camp to another. His reputation grew apace. The Boer leaders, most of whom had a mystic streak and an abiding faith in divine providence, consulted him regularly. General Hertzog (later a prime minister of the Union) noted in his diary after his first meeting with the clairvoyant: 'He foretold a successful battle near Wolmaranstad and described how the enemy would move.'

Van Rensburg remained quite untouched by the awe and respect which he inspired. But he was always solemnly insistent about the validity of his dreams, the rightness of his visions. As the South African Blue Book put it: 'He never attempted to exploit his gifts and he impressed most of those who came in contact with him with his apparent sincerity. If he duped others, it seemed he also duped himself. Moreover, and this was perhaps the secret of his continued success, his "visions" were invariably symbolic and mysterious; they possessed an adaptability of character that was truly Delphic.'

Of course, this is an ancient tradition—oracles were just as often traps as warnings, but at the same time it is strangely in accord with the Freudian theory of dreams, where almost everything is transformed into symbols and allusions which the psychoanalyst attempts to unravel. It must be said, however, that either the Boers were more adept at interpreting the dreams, or van Rensburg's prophecies must have been less hermetic and involved than those of Apollo and his colleagues.

It was he who helped General de la Rey to bring off one of the greatest Boer triumphs—the battle of Tweebos. Previously, the clairvoyant aided de la Rey to escape from an extremely dangerous position; shortly afterwards he gained the battle which led to the capture of a whole British force, including Field Marshal Lord Methuen. De la Rey became van Rensburg's grateful and close friend.

One of the most striking prophecies of van Rensburg was made shortly after the outbreak of World War I.

While the peace that Britain had imposed upon the conquered Boers was generally considered to be just and generous, the long South African conflict still left festering wounds, resentment and even hate. And though the majority of the citizens of the Union had little sympathy for the colonial ambitions of the Kaiser's empire, few of them were particularly eager to fight for British interests. Furthermore, many Boers thought that Germany would win.

For this, to a certain extent at least, the Transvaal seer was responsible, for he had recounted a dream which he had had many years before, and which was still remembered for its striking imagery. He had dreamt of a herd of bulls locked in stubborn and violent struggle. In the end it was a certain 'grey' bull which emerged the victor. Now, in 1914, those who recalled the prophetic vision, interpreted it in their own way: the bulls had represented the leading nations of Europe and the grey bull could be none but Germany.

If not entirely, yet to a large measure it was this dream—which Nicholaas van Rensburg refused to interpret—that gave the impetus to the rebellion the Boers planned, taking advantage of Britain's commitments in Europe and the heavy burden the defence of her far-flung empire represented. Among the leaders of the plot was General de la Rey. He, at least, had never forgotten how many hints the seer had given him of the 'great future' in front of him. One particularly vivid dream which he had recounted to his friend remained firmly fixed in the general's memory. Van Rensburg had first seen the number 15 against a dark cloud from which blood had been flowing. Then he saw de la Rey himself, 'returning home without a hat', followed by a carriage covered with flowers. Van Rensburg, when questioned, expressed his belief that his dream was the prophecy of great honour for the general.

De la Rey himself had spoken of this dream to several people—among them General Beyers, Commander-in-Chief of the Active Citizen Force of the Union, a kind of home-guard. But Beyers was also one of the secret leaders of the rebels, and he was just as much impressed by the dream as his friend de la Rey. He thought that the number 15 indicated a date—15 August 1914. So they called for that date a meeting at Treurfontein 'where the people would assemble and the Vierkleur—the national flag—would be hoisted'.

Afterwards the patriots would march to the frontier of German South West Africa where the Germans would provide them with arms and ammunition.

These ambitious plans never came to anything. The British found out about the plot and took precautions that frustrated the whole undertaking.

Beyers, however, was determined not to be thwarted. He organised another plot which was intended to lead to a general uprising, a much more dangerous affair than the failed conspiracy of 15 August. Once again he chose the 'Ides' of a month—this time it was to be 15 September—for he still firmly believed in van Rensburg's prophecy, though some of the logistics and preparations had to be adjusted to the modern times.

On this second 15th the Active Citizen Force—consisting of about 1,600 men—which was stationed at Potchefstroom was to rise against its British officers. The signal for the mutiny was to be the arrival of General Beyers and General de la Rey. Van Rensburg was issued with a special invitation—after all, it was only proper that he should be present when his prophecies reached fulfilment. But, rather disappointingly, he refused—excusing himself on the grounds that he did not yet see clearly where his path was leading. This, in itself, was a statement of precognition—for the seer never interpreted his own visions and their meaning was often as obscure to him as to those who acted on them.

On 14 September a car was dispatched from Potchefstroom to Johannesburg to pick up General de la Rey.

On the same night an escaped convict called Foster had been tracked down by the police, and traced to a hide-out in a suburb of Johannesburg. But just as the net was about to close, he slipped away in a stolen car. Immediately, all exits from the city were sealed and the police, fully armed, were stopping all cars.

There was one car that did not obey the order to halt. The police fired—and one passenger was mortally wounded, dying on the way to hospital. It was General de la Rey.

De la Rey's funeral was the tragic confirmation of van Rensburg's prophetic vision. He was indeed 'returning home without a hat'—in his coffin, followed by a carriage that was laden with the wreaths destined for his grave. There was a third eerie fact—the number of the room in the Johannesburg hotel whence he had set out for that fatal drive was . . . 15.

Mr Symonds reports that in the subsequent years van Rensburg had many other prophetic dreams, foretold innumerable events that came to pass. These included the devastating Spanish Influenza Epidemic of 1918 and the results of the General Election of 1924 in South Africa. He died in 1925 and the riddle of his gifts died with him.

Contemporary clairvoyants

In our own days there have been quite a number of clairvoyants whose exploits are well-documented, and while few have such a perfect record as the Transvaal seer, many of them have been and are aiding the police.

Marinus Bernardus Dykshoorn is probably the only one who has had his psychic status recognised even by the Dutch Passport Office. For his passport bears this entry:

Beroep/Profession/Occupation:
Helderziende. Clairvoyant

Yet Dykshoorn whose career stretches back over more than thirty years considers this an inadequate description. He says that the average clairvoyant's extra-sensory perceptions are restricted to *sight*—while his psychic gifts cover touch, taste, smell and hearing. And there is no word in English that would encompass all this.

He has solved some extremely complex crimes, has located graves that have been 'lost' since 1917, foretold a great many events that defied probability, and once tracked a thief in a distant country by telephone. His fame is solidly established in his native Holland and in a number of European countries. He has actually been licensed by the Dutch government authorities as a 'practitioner of the psychic arts'.

This was not an easy distinction to achieve. He had to pass a test by looking at blood samples on slides, giving the sex, age and other details of the persons from whom they were taken. He identified the first two quite easily. The third puzzled him somewhat—it seemed to be both male and female. He was quite right: it was a composite one and had been prepared to trick him. The fourth gave him an impression of a four-legged and furry animal. 'A dog,' he said. He was wrong—it was a fox. But that did not prevent him from getting his licence.

When he arrived in the United States with his wife and daughter in 1969 he lived for a while in Charlotte, North Carolina. There he was consulted by the state police about four different murder cases. In each case he was highly successful; but because, with the typically slow process of American court cases, they are all still *sub judice*, I have been asked not to publish their details. However, an important Charlotte businessman, an eye-witness of Dykshoorn's methods, provided an account for *The National Observer* which is a graphic description of the Dutchman's accomplishments.

In the middle of July 1970 a farmhouse burned to the ground with the owners, an elderly couple, perishing in the fire. At least so it was thought—until later when it was discovered that they had been shot before the fire was started. No other clues emerged, however, and Dykshoorn was called in.

He paced over the ruins of the house, manipulating the looped piano wire which serves him as a 'divining rod'. As he did, a strange change came over him—his manner of walking, his voice, his expression changed. He became another person.

A few moments later he began to act out a tragic sequence. A man came to the house, asked for a loan, was refused, fought, was hit on the nose and shot the elderly man and his wife. Dykshoorn finally reproduced the man's actions as he poured petrol over the floors and started the fire.

The Dutch seer's impersonation of the murderer was so life-like and detailed that those present had no difficulty in identifying a local resident.

But Dykshoorn continued. He traced the escape route, directed the police to the man's office and then to his home. A check at a local hospital showed that this same man had called there the day after the fire with an injured nose.

At this point the psychic retired from the case—and the police took over. There was an arrest and an indictment.

Dykshoorn's most spectacular European case involved a

man who phoned him from Germany and asked him to locate a missing boat. Dykshoorn cradled the phone between his chin and shoulder and swung his loop over a map of the area in Germany. He told his caller within a few minutes that his boat was 6 miles up a river.

A few hours later the same man telephoned again. He had found the boat—exactly where Dykshoorn had indicated. But a large sum of money which he, rather foolishly, had kept on board had vanished. The clairvoyant went to work again, then told his caller about another boat close to his where a man was preparing to sail. 'He has your money in a brown travelling bag,' he added.

The police arrested the man—and recovered the money exactly as specified. The grateful client naturally gave it the widest publicity and many newspapers and magazines published long articles about this extraordinary feat.

The Dutch psychic does not charge any fee for helping police officials or other authorities to solve or prevent crimes. He does charge, however, for private consultation. In 1972 he told a North Carolina widow that she would soon leave the state and that three nurses would take her apartment. She protested that this was nonsense, that she had a year's lease and no intention of going anywhere.

Two months later he received a letter from her with a Florida postmark: 'I was not only dispossessed from my apartment suddenly,' she wrote, 'but my brother unexpectedly invited me to live with him in Florida. I didn't want to tell you about it until I found out who moved into my old apartment. It was three nurses.'

There has been a long-enduring reluctance by the police in most countries to consult clairvoyants officially. This is easy to understand for their gifts have not received the endorsement of science and there is something sleazy and dishonest that clings to their reputations, something of the atmosphere of the fairground and the freak-show. But in recent years this attitude has rapidly changed, at least in some countries; and if the consultation is usually private and unofficial, success is acknowledged far less grudgingly and many police departments have established a regular, if slightly shamefaced relationship with psychics.

Irene F. Hughes, a good-looking blonde of Chicago, has been working with the police department of the city for more than ten years. She claims that her psychic powers are an inheritance from her Cherokee grandmother—and, according to the official records, they have certainly stood her in good stead, for she is credited with solving no less than fifteen murder cases for the Illinois police. Her fame has spread and now other police departments consult her regularly.

'Irene definitely does have clairvoyant powers,' Assistant Police Chief Virgin Jordan of the Kankakee, Illinois, Police Department stated in an interview given to Alan Markfield of the *National Enquirer*. 'I'm thoroughly convinced she has a deep perception—something that comes to her from some supernatural source.'

And Detective Sergeant William Chaney paid her this tribute: 'I can't thank her enough for the fine help she's given to the Kankakee Police Department. With her guidance and impressions we felt we were on the right track in an investigation.'

In 1964 a pretty girl of eighteen went for a walk one evening in Chicago—and disappeared. The police brought some of her clothing to Mrs Hughes, and spent three hours in her office while she 're-enacted the murder'.

She said that something heavy like a brick was used to crush her skull and that her body would be found under a tree near her home. She indicated the name and address of the murderer and added that the case would take a long time to solve.

She was right—it took almost three years. The murderer who tried to rape the girl and killed her when she resisted, had definitely lived at the address which Irene Hughes had given, but had moved and criss-crossed the country, seldom staying longer in one place than a day or two. In the end he was caught and convicted. A plaque on the wall of Mrs Hughes's office in Chicago bears witness to her aid—it is signed with the names of three policemen, thanking her for the leads she had given them in this case, and several others.

In the autumn of 1970 she was interviewed by Robert Cummings, a broadcaster for a Canadian station, about the kidnappings of the British diplomat James Cross and the Quebec cabinet minister Pierre LaPorte. (This sensational case mobilised a whole army of clairvoyants, some of which will be met with later.) Mrs Hughes forecast 6 November 1970 as the date when the first arrest would be made in the kidnapping investigation. She also predicted that the unfortunate LaPorte would be harmed, but that Cross would not be hurt. As we know, James Cross was released unharmed in the end, while LaPorte was found tied up and murdered in the boot of a car.

In March 1970 she produced the most rapid success of her career. It was a bitterly cold night and the police had been dragging a South Chicago Canal for the body of a victim of an accidental shooting. They could not find it. They called Mrs Hughes. She asked a detective where they had been looking and he told her: 'Over to the left.'

'No wonder you didn't find him,' the clairvoyant replied, 'the body's way over there under some rocks. It is coatless and one shoe is missing; he is wearing a white shirt. He'll be found before Sunday.'

Next morning—it was Thursday—a young man walking along the canal found the body, dressed exactly as Irene Hughes had 'seen' it. The dead man was discovered in a part of the general area which she had indicated but which the police had not yet searched.

Assistant Police Chief Jordan of Kankakee, who called on her many times, spoke of the occasion when she identified the killer of a policeman from more than twenty photographs of suspects. Because the victim was a policeman, the entire department felt that their honour was at stake. But though many of them gave up their days off, the concentrated investigation, lasting several weeks, had produced no results. At last Jordan called in Irene Hughes.

'My officers put the photos on the table, but Irene told them the person they were looking for wasn't there,' Jordan told Alan Markfield, 'so they laid down more photos. Then she said the man who did it was in that group but it was an old photo of him. She said he was a short, dark man who often wore an Army fatigue cap backwards. That description matched exactly a suspect we had in custody. During the same session she told one of the policemen that when he got home he would find some shocking news about his father. When he did return to his house, he was told his father had been flown to Houston Hospital with a heart attack. She told the other policeman that when he got home he would find someone he least expected to see. And when he did, there was his sister from California . . .'

The man in the Army fatigue cap later confessed and was convicted.

Often the police brought her the clothes or other belongings of a missing person—for this provided her with the clue for psychometry. 'I'll hold the clothes when I am alone and quiet and meditate. Then I'll write down the impressions I get,' Irene explained when a policewoman gave her a bundle of clothing belonging to a boy who had vanished.

Her 'hits' are remarkably frequent and while she has no theory or explanation for her psychic talents, she is one of the comparatively few clairvoyants who have a lasting and effective relationship with the police authorities.

Another lady blessed with 'second sight' bore the unusual name of Reverent Gwen and lived in Hamilton, Ontario. (She died in the late sixties, aged eighty-five.) As Earl Butler, a Hamilton resident, related, she helped a great many people during her lifetime. Once Mr Butler himself turned to her in a serious family dilemma. Earl Butler's son had died in 1960 and when his papers were examined by his widow, it was found that some documents in connection with his life insurance were missing and might have been stolen. The younger Mrs Butler searched everywhere in the house but could not find any trace of them. Her father-in-law then telephoned Mrs Reverent Gwen and explained the details; she asked him to give her until next day to provide the answer. When he phoned again, she told him that the papers had not been stolen but were mislaid—packed away with some bedlinen and could be found between two sheets in a drawer of a bureau in one of the bedrooms. Mr Butler sr immediately called his daughter-in-law, and waited on the phone while she went to look. The missing papers were found exactly in the place indicated by the medium. On another occasion, again using the same method, she helped Mr Butler to trace some important pictures which his wife had lost. On several cases she located missing persons and gave the Ontario police considerable help in problems that had baffled them.

A third clairvoyant, Mrs Beverly C. Jaegers, mother of six, has organised a whole group of psychics in St Louis. It is called the 'Psychical Research and Training Center' and she seems to have very ambitious plans to mobilise the gifts which she and her associates are supposed to possess. In February 1973 she reported: 'There is a group here of fifteen *trained* psychics who are working on crime cases and disappearances constantly. All but two of them are my own trained students. The others are "natural" psychics.

'I am in the process of setting up a "chain" of psychics across the United States who will be on call at any time in case we are working on something involving the area in which they live. If it does, then they will be put on to the "scent" and will feed results to me here as co-ordinator of the operation. Nothing like this has ever been done before to my knowledge, and I think it will be of great aid in more ways than one. We can only work with reputable people and so must check them out through our tools of handwriting-analysis (one of us is a graphoanalyst), astrology (our own Diana Bills is the newly elected head of ASAP) and psychometry . . .'

In September 1971 the *St Louis Globe-Democrat* carried a long story about one of Mrs Jaegers's own cases.

A Mrs Sally Lucas had disappeared and Mrs Jaegers was consulted as to her whereabouts. She was on her way to a vacation in Florida. Later her car was found being driven by a man called Anthony Damico who was charged with her murder—but of the body there was no trace.

The day before Damico's arrest, Mrs Jaegers was given a powder puff and a nightgown belonging to Mrs Lucas. Later she was consulted by the police and sat in the car. There she wrote down or dictated her clairvoyant impressions. Next day Mrs Lucas's body was found. It is interesting to compare the psychic's statements with the facts as later established: 'Pain, right side of head and neck, a feeling like a cut, impression of a small person, medium length hair, not a heavy smoker, female . . .'

(Sally Lucas was struck the mortal blow on the right side of her head. She was a moderate smoker, 5ft tall and wore her hair medium length.)

'Impression of men in uniform (police) bending over looking into a car, near water.'

(The next morning Sally Lucas's car was discovered in Florida, near water, and was examined by police at the scene.)

'I have the feeling she will not be found alive . . . My deepest impressions are that the woman will be found in or near water.'

(Sally Lucas was found dead, in a dried-out creek bed which would normally contain water but did not in 1971 because of excessive drought.)

Mrs Jaegers also received impressions of the numbers 3 and 4, which were part of the car licence plate of Sally Lucas. The time she disappeared was between 3 and 4pm.

While in the car, Mrs Jaegers added some further details: 'Head hurt—hit water again—man dragging a body. Time near 4.47 . . . Bridge is very near . . .'

(The body was found about 50yd from a small bridge.)

On other minor points she proved to be right—while in some details she was inaccurate. But, among other things, she also felt the initial C strongly and got impressions of an aeroplane.

(The body was found not far from the Spirit of St Louis Airport and much closer to Highways C and CC.)

She repeated the words 'horse' and 'horse's head' several times.

(The body was found near the edge of Wild Horse Creek road.)

As for the killer she spoke of his 'infantile mind'; someone who 'boasts about plans and takes credit for things he hasn't done . . . This was not a robbery—the motive was sexual but twisted . . . He plans things at night. He walks in alleys at night. He loves the night.'

All this fitted Anthony Damico fairly closely.

In February 1973 Mrs Jaegers was working with the police on two cases, one involved a missing boy in northern Iowa, the other, a similar disappearance in the St Louis, Missouri area. Sometimes she inevitably reached a dead end—as in a burglary case involving a famous painting that had been removed from the district—and an investment fraud case on which she had co-operated with local detectives, which did not result in an indictment. She certainly seems to be a most active lady who actually teaches a night-course in psychometry at the St Louis University City School of Continuing Education.

One of the most striking cases of psychic and police co-operating was that of Olof Jonsson who was born in Malmø, Sweden, but who has been living for the past twenty years in the United States. His story has been very fully told in Brad Steiger's *The Psychic Feats of Olof Jonsson* and *Fate* has published several extracts from the book.

Olof was trained as an engineer; during World War II he served in the Swedish merchant marine. After 1945 when he was in his late twenties, several Swedish parapsychologists, including Dr John Bjorkhelm, Professor Olle Holmberg, and Sven Turck tested his psychic talents by extensive experiments. In America he has worked with Professor J. B. Rhine, J. G. Pratt, Edward Cox and Ian Stevenson. He achieved nationwide fame in the States when he conducted some ESP tests with astronaut Edward Mitchell. He lives today in a southern suburb of Chicago and works for an engineering firm; he has an American wife.

The most striking case which Brad Steiger relates in Olof Jonsson's career began in March 1952 when a Malmø journalist named Leif Sunde telephoned him. Sunde had been present at a number of experiments which Jonsson had conducted in Varberg and elsewhere.

The journalist began by referring to the events in Tjornarp where a mass-murderer had claimed thirteen victims. The police had no leads, but this was hardly surprising as the killer finished off his victims and then set fire to the house, thereby destroying most of the clues. Whether he was a sex maniac or had some other motive, remained a riddle.

Jonsson reacted almost at once. 'He robs them,' he told Sunde. 'He—and it *is* a man—murders, then robs. He does not sexually violate his victims. And he has killed both men and women. Is that correct?'

Sunde said, yes, there have been male victims—but more women than men. He had been assigned to cover the story and he wondered whether Jonsson would be willing to work with him. He had already checked with the investigating police officer in Tjornarp and had obtained his consent to bring the psychic into the case.

For Olof Jonsson this was a critical moment. Though he had been tested his clairvoyant powers in laboratories, on board ship when sailing through mine-infested waters, though he had given private séances, he had never been involved with crime detection. He was a man who hated violence. Could he project his mind into that of a sadistic murderer?

As he hesitated, he had a clear, terrifying vision. He saw flames flickering in a corner of his own home. A woman sprawled, bleeding, clutching her stomach, mortally wounded but not yet dead. The fire reached her feet. Her clothing apparently had been saturated with some combustible liquid and now burst into flames. Her screams were inhuman, echoing in Olof's ears.

Shaken, terrified, he told the journalist that he would come to Tjornarp and would do his best to bring the criminal to justice.

He phoned his sister, Mrs Birgit Persson, and told her about the appeal for help. She protested at first that it would be a shattering, perhaps dangerous experience for him, and in the end suggested that she should accompany him. This was something Olof very much wanted for he knew he could draw mental and moral support from her which he needed.

When the party of four, including Sunde and his photographer, Erling Tollefsen, arrived in Tjornarp, some 40 miles from Malmø, having travelled in Sunde's car, they were received warmly by the police and within a short time were being shown the various murder sites by a young police officer, assigned to help them in every possible way.

As they stood in the middle of the ashes of such a place, Olof shuddered and whispered: 'God! It was terrible . . .'

He had 'seen' blood and pain, but not the murderer's face. Officer Hedin, who was their escort, asked insistent questions —but Jonsson said that the images had been faint, that he could not tell him anything. They had dinner together and then Hedin excused himself, saying that he had to meet a young lady who was a very important person in his life. As he left, Sunde said: 'What an earnest and co-operative young officer! He stands there so patiently while you soak up the impressions of each site, Olof. He will be a great help to you . . .'

The young engineer seemed to be jolted out of some deep reverie. 'Yes,' he said, 'he will be of great assistance . . .'

For two days they continued going from place to place. On the third day Hedin handed Olof the charred remains of a rifle and explained that it was found in the ruins of a house in which a woman was killed. 'Her friends had been positive that she did not own one, though it had not been established whether the murderer had used it.

Birgit protested that it should have been presented earlier—the only physical clue that had been offered until then. But Olof only asked for a few moments' silence. Again, the images started to swirl almost at once—violent and brutal.

When it was over, Jonsson asked to be driven back to the hotel.

'Did you see the murderer?' asked Leif Sunde. 'Can you tell us anything about him?'

'Don't keep us in suspense,' Officer Hedin added his plea. He had stayed close to the young psychic. 'Tell us what you saw.'

'I've seen nothing,' Olof said in a low voice. 'But please, I would like to rest.'

When they got back to the Tjornarp hotel, Jonsson locked himself in his room and lay down on the bed. For a few seconds he relaxed, trying to achieve the proper frame of mind—a 'feeling of harmony' which he needed to summon up the psychic images from whatever part of his mind, his subconscious, or outside source that they might come. And he began to 'visit' the scenes of the murders—as they were before the houses or homes had been reduced to ashes.

First he saw a tall, young, blonde woman, reading in an armchair. There was a knock on the door. Her face showed surprise and puzzlement, but not fear—she obviously knew and trusted her caller. She asked him in. Was it some official business—or . . . And then, her eyes widening in startled amazement, she saw the rifle . . .

Next—a redheaded woman preparing the evening meal for her husband and children who were on an outing. The doorbell went. She was cross at being interrupted—was it her husband he wanted to see? And then the explosion, the sudden, searing pain . . .

A large, plump man—his spectacles being shattered as half his face was blown off . . .

A woman, just out of her teens, living on her own, having recently left her parents' home. She put up a fight before her life ebbed away . . .

In a ghastly and gory parade Olof Jonsson viewed all the thirteen victims. Every one of them was killed with that rifle which Officer Hedin had made him hold; and each time he saw the same ice-cold eyes sighting along the barrel; the same set features relaxing into a cruel smile.

At last, exhausted and yet with a strange calmness, the psychic unlocked his door and asked his sister, the journalist and the photographer to enter. He wanted to know where Hedin was. Tollefsen explained that he had been called away. Should they call the precinct and ask him to return before Olof would make a statement?

'No,' said the clairvoyant. 'Lock the door.'

When they all sat down around the bed, he added quietly: 'The murderer—it is Officer Hedin.'

Birgit gasped. The two men looked sceptical. 'Are you sure?' the journalist asked.

'Yes. I saw him pulling the trigger as soon as he handed me the rifle. Of course, I couldn't say anything at the time. If I had, he would have killed us all—I read murder in his mind. You remember—we were miles out in the country—it would have been easy to dispose of us . . .'

'Surely only a madman would have taken such a risk . . .'

'He *is* mad. He has killed and robbed thirteen people. He burned their houses in order to cover his outrageous actions. Four extra lives would have meant nothing to him.'

Sunde was still unable to accept it. 'B-but . . . he has been so helpful. He never left us since we arrived . . .'

'For very good reasons. We must now phone his superiors

and tell them that their most efficient and helpful officer is a psychopathic killer.'

'But Olle,' Birgit shook her head, 'how can you make them believe you? What proof have you, except your second sight? It won't be easy to persuade them that a police officer is a murderer.'

'I must try,' Jonsson shrugged. 'I know I am right.'

Leif Sunde undertook to call the police station and ask somebody to come to the hotel. When he returned to Olof's room, he looked puzzled and shaken.

'They told me they'd be glad to come over but asked us to be a little patient. Officer Hedin has disappeared—they are afraid that he might be the killer's most recent victim.'

But when Hedin's body was found in the river the next day it was obvious that he had committed suicide. In his home the police found a note confessing the murders, and saying that he knew that it was only a question of time before the psychic from Malmø would unmask his guilt.

His death depressed Olof for though it ended the mass murders, he felt that he could have somehow helped the man with the sick mind before he killed himself. 'He committed his crimes,' he explained, 'because his girl-friend had made extravagant demands on him—asked for gifts and outings he could not afford on his modest salary. That's why he needed the money which he took from his victims. And after the second or the third, killing became easy for him, for his conscience had died . . .'

In March 1973 American newspapers revealed the story of the co-operation between the Freeport (Maine) Police Department and Alex Tanous, a young psychic of East Millonocket, Maine. Herman Boudreau, the Freeport police chief, gave him full credit for helping to solve the puzzling and brutal killing of an eight-year-old Freeport boy, John A. Nason.

The boy had disappeared from his home on 13 June 1972 and was later found strangled. The police were making little headway until Chief Boudreau heard of Tanous and his earlier successes. The parents and relatives of the dead boy also wanted him to be consulted.

'This was the first time I had used Tanous in a case', Herman Boudreau told the press, 'but I have always felt there must be something in ESP. I thought: a lot of big-town police experts listen to psychics, so why shouldn't the police chief in a little town do the same? I'd go to any length to solve a case. I'd listen to anybody if it would help. And Tanous did help us—tremendously. I would definitely use him again.'

The first thing Chief Boudreau wanted to know whether the psychic's impressions and views backed up what the police investigation was showing. They were concentrating on four key suspects at the time though they did not tell Tanous this. He was taken through the apartment house where the boy lived and then they drove him around the district. This was repeated several times. But whenever they left the apartment house, Tanous would say: 'No, no!' and would continue pointing back to the boy's home. So the chief took him back for another look.

The psychic stood unmoving and then began to speak, telling the policemen that the boy was dead, that the body was in the apartment house—though he couldn't tell them exactly where—and that the body was wrapped in something and under something.

Next day Tanous called at the chief's office.

'He handed me a sketch that he said he had drawn in the car coming over,' Herman Boudreau later told the reporters. 'When I saw it, I immediately pulled out a photograph of

Milton I. Wallace, one of our suspects in the case. And you couldn't tell the difference. To someone knowing Wallace, and seeing the sketch . . . well, they would have known they were one and the same person straight off . . .'

There was no way, the police chief added, in which Tanous could have known about Wallace. A Freeport shoe factory worker, he lived only a few doors away from the missing boy, on the same floor of the apartment house.

The police had already talked to him. Wallace had a record—he had been in prison for a sex assault on a seven-year-old boy—and they didn't like his story. But the sketch by Tanous was one of the things that made Chief Boudreau decide on the ninth day of the investigation to 'take a chance' and charge Wallace with the crime. They went to his apartment, and found the boy's decomposed body under a bed, wrapped in a blanket, exactly as Tanous had suggested.

Wallace was convicted of the crime and sentenced to life imprisonment on 15 December 1972.

Success and failure

Obviously, as in many other occult fields, the successes get the publicity and the failures are forgotten. But in these cases statistics and ratios of failure and success do not count much. Psychics are rarely called in unless the police have come to a dead end, have failed to turn up adequate clues. But, especially in the United States, in the Netherlands and in Scandinavia, they are being consulted more and more often.

There is still a good deal of argument whether the clairvoyants involved in the lurid Boston Strangler case were right or wrong. The strangler, of course, was never tried—

he made a peculiar sort of deal with the prosecution and was apparently allowed to live out his days in a psychiatric hospital. But the number of examples of regular and extensive collaboration between clairvoyants and police is certainly growing—and every year there are dozens of stories to tell. Perhaps it would be worthwhile to involve them in fighting the political terrorism of different ideologies and groupings, from Black September to Black Panthers, from Provos to neo-Nazis. If second sight could save a single life, locate the letter-bombs, remove the explosive from the luggage compartment of an aircraft, the limpet mine from a ship, it would be a new opening, a fresh approach to the use of the power that, still unexplored and still unmeasured, ferments and functions in the human brain. To deny the existence of this power is just as short-sighted as to ascribe to it supernatural origins—but, in any case, to ignore its practical applications has become old-fashioned and wasteful.

4
PENDULUM, ROD AND BOARD

For many centuries it has been the dream of men to utilise their subconscious, extra-sensory perceptions for the discovery of precious metals, hidden treasures or water under the earth. The dispute still rages as to whether this is possible and whether the undeniable results achieved by dowsers and diviners have been due to accident or some occult power. But the sceptics seem to be on the losing end.

. . . *Autobahn accident rate reduced* Between 1960 and 1966 26 accidents occurred along the Vienna–Salzburg Autobahn, all of them near Linz, at kilometre-stone 120.5. One motorist was killed and in 16 of the accidents no reason for the crash could be found. A retired chemist, Rudolf Wenger, went over the ground with a divining rod and discovered three underground streams. He claimed that these sent out rays, affecting the people and making them react without realising it. He asked for permission to plant three loops of what he called special metal on the danger spot. Georg Hofer, one of the Autobahn executives, told him to go ahead for he and his colleagues were certain the metal loops could do no harm. Another official said: 'We would have buried dead dogs if it would help to cut down the accident rate.' Whatever the reason—between 1966 and 1969 only 8 accidents occurred, all of them due to weather conditions or to human error. A drop of almost 80 per cent.

Town relies on 'smeller', finds water In a report from Lancaster, Pennsylvania, the United Press describes how the little town of Mountville relies on a 'water smeller' to find its water. Seventy-three-year-old George Keck, a stocky farmer, left his native Germany in 1926, and now works for the Lancaster Area Sewer Authority, telling them when the sewer line they are excavating is about to hit a water line. He does this by carrying a pair of chrome-plated pliers. When he passes over a water line or underground stream, the pliers seem to be almost yanked from his hands. Mountville's public works director, John Hess, often calls on Keck's services; he is a firm believer in the old gentleman's powers. Keck discovered his unusual powers when he was twelve. During a drought he happened to try his pliers and found water. But he can also use a peach twig—'as long as it is alive'.

Dowsing Society 'finds' plenty of fresh water under Mt Gleason The Southern California Edison Company has a 'water witcher' on its payroll. His name is Jerry Smith and his official title is 'agricultural sales representative' from the company's San Bernardino's office. He uses a 2ft rod with a slight curve in the middle. He has found more than 8,000 wells in the last two decades. The company supports him for a sound business reason—the people for whom he finds the wells usually pump the water electrically. The Southern California Chapter of the American Society of Dowsers, as reported in August 1970, claims to have found enough fresh water under Mt Gleason, 10 miles north of La

Canada (above Los Angeles), to meet the needs of Southern California throughout this century. They have done it by 'map dowsing', using a small pendulum hung on a chain.

Truck driver with bent stick locates sewer after engineers with electronic equipment fail After experts with electronic equipment and a mine detector spent hours trying to find the location of an old sewer under a town's streets and failed, along came Fred Fell, a lorry driver, who found the sewer in a few minutes with a divining rod. Graham Peatty, who headed the team of engineers in Southam, Warwickshire, explained: 'Our modern equipment had done nothing but he was able to pinpoint the sewer effortlessly. He came with a forked branch taken from a hazel tree and then walked back and forth across the street twelve times. The rod shuddered and twisted to a point on the street and we dug there. He had found the exact spot where the sewer crossed the road and he was able to show us the exact line the sewer took under the street. We are very grateful, but don't ask me to explain it.'

These are just four recent examples of the dowser's achievements, which, according to official science, should not have happened. For the United States Geological Survey stated: 'A variety of researchers, through controlled experiments, have shown conclusively that water-witching is not a reliable method of locating ground water.' And *Nature*, reporting a recent study in which dowsers were matched against non-dowsers in finding buried objects and water, came to the conclusion: 'The results obtained for dowsing are no more reliable than a series of guesses.'

The dowsers respond to these sceptics by saying that if you *believe* dowsing works, it will usually work for you. But if you approach it with doubt, the results will be negative. (This, of course, is a frequent excuse or alibi of clairvoyants, materialisation, voice mediums and faith healers if they fail.) But the spokesmen for the 'water-witches' and diviners insist that there has to be a tremendous need and desire before dowsing will work in most cases. (No doubt, the Southam engineers accumulated such a 'tremendous need and desire' to find that sewer.)

The champions of pendulum and rod maintain that American soldiers in Vietnam used coat hangers to locate enemy mines and tunnels and that dowsing was taught at several Marine Corps bases. The craft has been used for centuries but, the believers in the practice say, 'hardly ever does anyone admit it for fear of ridicule'. Even Albert Einstein has been reputed to have been a life-long devotee of the practice—though there is no reliable confirmation of this claim.

Ground water geologists whose professional task it is to locate water supplies have nothing but open scorn for dowsers; they refuse to believe that underground water exists anywhere in quantities the diviners claim to have discovered. According to them 'underground water is merely water that has fallen from the sky as rain or snow and formed into subterranean pools'.

On the other hand Dr Delaney, Professor of Philosophy and lecturer on ESP at Loyola University, subscribes to the Jungian theory that 'when man is able to turn off his reasoning, analytical mind, he is then able to tune in his subconscious'. While there is a lack of scientific proof for dowsing, Dr Delaney has found that 'the force field—in other words, the beliefs of onlookers—can greatly affect a psychic performance' which is readily applicable to dowsing.

Thus, as in every field of the occult, the battle-lines are drawn, both sides have been able to marshal arguments in their own support—and the judgement of the unbiased third parties must be reserved.

Dowsers of many lands

It is almost three centuries since Monsieur Royer, a Rouen attorney, published his *Traité des influences et des vertus occultes des êtres terrestres* (Treatise about the influences and occult qualities of mundane beings). The book, which appeared in 1677, had several references to the possibility of using the divining rod to catch thieves and murderers. Sixteen years later de Vallemont in his book *La physique occulte* described in great detail how the tracks of criminals were followed with the divining rod; the illustration on the title page of the book showed Justice holding, in place of her usual scales, a forked twig. In the centuries that have passed we still have not succeeded in clearing up the riddle of the divining rod; but at least science, however negative its attitude, has accepted these phenomena as subjects worthy of investigation. For or against, more exact results have been achieved than some 150 years ago when the Munich Academy of Sciences commissioned its physicist members to examine the matter.

The Old Testament relates how Moses smote the rock and provided water for the people of Israel who were dying of thirst. This means, of course, that the alleged ability of the divining rod to indicate underground water-courses was already known in the dim past and it is not surprising when on a clay-tablet of Nineveh we find depicted a goddess called 'The Mistress of the Magic Staff'. The Scythians and Tartars practised rhabdomancy, divination by rods or wands, and it was the same practice that inspired the plaintive cry of the Prophet Hosea: 'My people ask counsel at their stocks and their staff declareth unto them.' Tacitus mentioned that the Germans used the same methods and the word 'to divine' (*wünschen*) was at one time the equivalent of 'to practise magic' (*zaubern*). Out of this the divining rod or *Wünschelrute* derived. It is mentioned in the great epic, the Nibelung Song, where the dowsing rod is of pure gold and it is stated that the owner of such a rod is 'master of everyone all over the world'. The lore of the divining rod which helped to find buried treasure, veins of silver and gold and underground springs, was developed, treasured and passed on from generation to generation—especially among miners. They considered a forked twig or hazel, cut on Midsummer Night under special rites and magic spells, the most suitable for such work; the rod was held in both hands at the end of the forks while the handle of the rod stood up and could move to point at the hiding place of the treasure or water—or at the miscreant whose identity was being sought.

One of the most enlightened spirits of the seventeenth century, Athanasius Kircher, inventor of the magic lantern, teacher of mathematics and Hebrew at the College of Rome (before devoting himself to the study of hieroglyphics and archaeology), spoke of the possibility of discovering hidden things with the divining rod and of 'aiding the pursuit of criminals' as an established fact. He called it '*virgula divina*'. At the beginning of the eighteenth century long and learned tomes were published about the subject, trying to explain the movement of the rod by the influence of tiny 'bodies' exuded by the hidden objects or by the Cartesian 'little elementals'. Equally, the theory was developed that in the flesh of 'people of evil' such forces or miniature bodies existed and these attracted the divining rod. Italian and German physicists attempted to examine and analyse the reported cases. They arrived at the theory of a special 'electrometric power' which was supposed to be awakened in particularly sensitive persons by veins of metal or moving water underground. This influence was supposed to manifest itself not only through the movements of the rod or twig held in the hand but also in physical sensations—even in violent convulsions. Campetti, the Italian dowser, acquired international fame. He participated in the Munich experiments at the beginning of the nineteenth century and used not only twigs but also the 'bipolar scales', a piece of coal or pyrite suspended on a thread which was supposed to start moving under the influence of hidden metals or running water. (This approach was revived in the telekinetic experiments conducted in Scandinavia, the USSR and the United States, trying to move a pendulum or other suspended metal subjects by a medium's concentrated thought. Quite notable, though still inexplicable results were achieved under laboratory conditions.)

In 1905 it caused quite a sensation in Germany when well-known and serious scientists began to occupy themselves with the problems of dowsing, and even official circles took an interest in them. When the Kaiser's Reich prepared the colonisation of German South West Africa and the native geologists could not solve the vital problem of an adequate water supply, William II intervened and sent Herr von Usler, an agricultural adviser to Africa. In two years of extremely arduous work he succeeded in finding wells and streams at almost 800 different places. In about 60 per cent of the dowsing indications they found water in the exact spot; in about a quarter of the sites the data given by von Usler as to the depth of the necessary boring were also found to be correct.

But Usler fulfilled another task during these two years—something for which he had not been trained but which proved extremely useful. The Germans discovered that there was an immense amount of pilfering during the construction of their buildings and other installations. It was almost impossible to stop it for they did not have sufficient men to guard the stockpiles and store-rooms. One of the old African hands then suggested that every morning when the workers were paraded the agricultural counsellor should be present—and should use his dowsing rod to pick out the culprits or suspects. Von Usler did not really believe that this would be useful but he agreed to make a 'trial run', and his divining rod behaved most gratifyingly. When the hut of the first worker—actually a foreman—was searched (the rod had reacted to him almost instantaneously) a large quantity of pilfered material was discovered. The 'inspection by divining rod' continued for three days—after which all thefts ceased.

During World War I dowsers were used for special purposes—especially after an Austrian, Colonel Karl Beichl, succeeded in locating Serbian mines in the Danube and Sava rivers with his divining rod. This sort of 'psychic mine detection' seemed to become obsolete when modern mine-detectors were developed and proved about 70 per cent effective. But we have already mentioned that in Vietnam, at least, the GIs revived it. Also during the 1914–18 war, Major Otto von Grave was able to find water in the Sinai desert when both engineers and geologists had failed to do so. He used the divining rod and subsequent borings, carried out by the British, confirmed his claims. Today the Israelis employ the same, though somewhat improved, methods with equal success in the Negev and elsewhere.

While the divining rod produces certain movements about different underground formations, quite often the rod does *not* react when there are established deposits of metals or bodies of water under the surface. This applies, too, to the Siderian scales which were used in former times for fortune-telling tricks and were favourite instruments of medieval miners for exploring metals. The pendulum was used by letting a gold ring swing on a thread above a metal vessel which had the letters of the alphabet etched along its rim at equal distance from each other (an early version of the ouija board). The letters over which it swung were written down and combined into words. Another form of the Siderian scales' use was hydromancy—letting the ring swing over a container filled with holy water and jotting down the letters (which were repeated aloud) at which the ring stopped swinging or oscillated violently—here, too, the combination of such letters provided the oracle.

Karl Reichenbach, the German natural scientist and industrialist (1788–1869), the discoverer of creosote and paraffin in wood tar, also conducted researches in what he called *od*, an alleged power or natural force which, he claimed, produced the phenomena of hypnotism. Reichenbach was a highly trained and accurate observer—even if he sometimes drew the wrong conclusions from his observations. He thought that the Siderian scales represented a natural phenomenon of 'the highest possible scientific importance' and prophesied a 'brilliant future' for their use. He claimed that a suspended ring, hanging about three inches above a body or substance, described definite circular movements according to the chemical nature of the body—for instance, it moved in a circle in the presence of gold and in an ellipse above silver; the circle, in his view, corresponded to the male and the ellipse to the female principle. Reichenbach assumed that all bodies gave off 'an emanation' which did not reduce their weight, could pass through glass and had a motive influence upon the pendulum. Photographs and handwriting were supposed to excite similar movements of the scales and if held above the photographs of sick people, the experimenter holding the pendulum was said to feel pains in his arms and even have trouble with his breathing. The German scientist applied the same principles to crime detection and though he found little sympathy among the police authorities of his own country, he worked out an elaborate system by which criminal tendencies and actual crimes committed could be established; his system was somewhat similar to Lombroso's typology though he based it on the reaction of the pendulum rather than on physical, inherited characteristics.

Divining rods and Siderian scales belong to the same group of phenomena—yet experiments with the scales do not seem to require any special talent while dowsing demands definite natural gifts. A pendulum held in the hand swings, no matter what body provides its alleged 'radiations'. I have witnessed a great many experiments and have found that the composition of the test matter has no influence upon the manner of the movement, which is always transmitted by the hand holding the Siderian scales. All the various pretty conclusions drawn from the differences in the movements are founded on illusions. I myself have succeeded in producing circular movements above a gold watch and elliptical ones above a silver watch—*provided I know which metal they are composed of*; nor did I feel at the time that I was consciously influencing the pendulum. Once I took several photographs and wrapped them in opaque paper, placing them under the pendulum. The reaction was more or less the same regardless of the photographs being of men or women, adults or babies. It was the same with jewellery in closed boxes; the movements of the Siderian scales were either circular or elliptical, without any system or pattern. More often than not they began as circular and then slipped into elliptical patterns.

The similarity of the movements of the dowsing rod and the pendulum points to the fact that even with the divining rod the movements originate in the hand holding it.

Times have passed when people laughed at the dowsers'

craft and considered them as impractical dreamers or ridiculous enthusiasts. In the United States, the late Kenneth Roberts, the distinguished novelist, started a whole campaign to change the general attitude of scientists and laymen—but this, as we have seen from some of the press reports I have quoted, was hardly necessary. There is, of course, no reason to become involved in all the flights of imagination, all the foolish theories which the partisans of dowsing and Siderian scales develop and champion. How could one accept the claim that a pendulum drew the same individual curves over the *shadows* of a man as over the man himself, or that the pendulum stopped completely over the hearts of the photographs of dead people? Perhaps the claim that the Siderian scales could be helpful in diagnosing diseases is more serious—though one must qualify this with many reservations. Then there is the finding of lost objects, the examination of forged documents—pendulum and rod have even been employed in trying to establish the authorship of pictures and to discover fakes. It is said that they have a special rôle in finding people buried alive and as primitive Geiger counters in tracing radioactive minerals with the help of good photographs.

But all this is apt to be much exaggerated and misused. Certainly, divining rod and Siderian scales have the great advantage that one can experiment with them without cost or trouble; they can be produced by the simplest means and allow everybody (as the Viennese dowser Hans Falkinger and many others have shown) to practise, without laboratory training, the difficult art of objective observation. There is a special attraction in following on walks (or even in your own room) the interesting phenomena which these two primitive instruments are able to produce and to study forces of nature which are little discussed at school or college. Goethe's saying about 'Nature not yielding her secrets in broad daylight' is not quite true but without any complex apparatus, or esoteric knowledge, one can gather new experiences and reach honest satisfaction. All this amateur dowsers have discovered and for this reason alone, the divining rod and the Siderian scales are bound to survive and even flourish in our modern age.

The sceptics

A Dutch geologist, Professor S. W. Tromp, spent ten years trying to prove that dowsing and the use of divining rods, Siderian scales, pendulums and other similar apparatus was a total waste of time. At the end of the decade he published a monumental book called *Psychical Physics* with the long-established and distinguished firm of Elsevier. In it he came to three startling conclusions. The first was that there existed a human sensitivity to underground water and that it could be demonstrated by experiments. Secondly, that most people did possess such sensitivity, at least to some degree. And thirdly, that it could be explained scientifically without invoking 'second sight'.

He used a professional diviner whom he blindfolded and whose ears were plugged with cotton wool. He was led near an electric apparatus while holding a twig in the divining position. When sufficient current was switched on to set up a weak magnetic field, the tip of the twig jerked sharply downwards. This suggested that the diviner had some hitherto unrecorded sensitivity. Tests with other diviners, using bent wires instead of twigs, showed that they could also detect minute changes in the strength of the magnetism round them. The professor claimed similar results when minute electric currents were applied to a diviner's skin.

A portable heart-beat recorder was used to make charts

of a diviner's reactions when he passed over underground water, and they established that the human body unconsciously detected some sensation whether a 'magic' rod was carried or not. Professor Tromp suggested that some physical force related to the presence of underground water influenced the body through the skin. This affected the nervous system which in turn made the muscles twitch. The rod served to magnify this movement and put the forearm muscles under tension. Tromp rated the skin as the likeliest detector because a diviner's sensitivity seemed to depend on the electrical resistance of his skin; any diviner, for example, could increase his sensitivity by rinsing his hands in salt water or weak sulphuric acid.

Diviners did better when their skin was well insulated from the soil by thick-soled boots. They put up a poor show bare-footed.

All this seemed a straightforward enough explanation. But then one of the dowsers whom the professor had used, a Fleming named Victor G from Ghent, did something that went far beyond Tromp's modest and matter-of-fact conclusions. Two brutal murders had been committed in a small village between Ghent and Antwerp. Victor G was unaware of them because he had been very ill, unable to read, listen to the radio or even receive visitors. When he was getting a little better, he picked up his divining rod—much as someone returning to life after a debilitating sickness might pick up his favourite fishing rod or golf club as a reminder that he is back in the land of the living—but as he held it, quite slack, in his hand, the rod began to quiver and point. It pointed at the floor where Madame G had spread some newspapers over the carpet to protect it from spilled water —for her husband had to have frequent rub-downs and cold compresses as ordered by the doctor.

So insistent was the hazel twig which G used for his

experiments with Professor Tromp that he called for his wife and insisted that she should remove the paper from the floor. As she did, the rod began to perform a frantic dance and flew from the ailing man's hand, landing with its point indicating the headline: POLICE BAFFLED IN MURDER INVESTIGATION. With his wife's help, G retrieved his hazel twig and, for the first time, read the two-day-old account of the latest developments in the murder case—which consisted mainly of reports of police bafflement.

Though Madame G protested, the dowser got out of bed, dressed and had himself driven to the Ghent police headquarters. He had considerable difficulty in being admitted to the presence of the chief inspector in charge of the case, but as, in his 'non-psychic' life, he was a respected businessman, he managed to do so in the end. Even when he told the high-ranking police officer about the strange behaviour of a hazel twig, he was asked whether he wasn't suffering from hallucinations—perhaps an after-effect of his illness? G did not take the jibe amiss; he asked to be taken to the room in which a large-scale map of Ghent and its environs had been put up; the progress—or rather the lack of it—in the police enquiries was marked with drawing pins. Because of the circumstances of the killings it was agreed that the murderer or murderers must live within a certain area and the pins marked the streets which had been already checked by the police—without any positive results.

The chief inspector agreed to G's request—the more readily because the businessman couldn't have possibly known of the existence of the map. Nor did he protest when his caller produced his divining rod. After a few seconds' immobility, the hazel twig began to react. It pointed unerringly at a street *outside* the area marked on the map. The chief inspector smiled and said that this must be a mistake—the police had cordoned off the area, no one could have escaped, nobody but officials were allowed to move in and out of the place. But G insisted—and in the end he was dispatched with a police car and a detective.

The house was empty—but a search disclosed the murder weapon, a carving knife. It had been wrapped in a small towel, and these two objects were sufficient to track down the murderer, an assistant chef in one of the local hotels, a psychopath who later confessed to three earlier murders that had never been cleared up.

G went back to his sickbed where he spent another two weeks before fully recovering.

A somewhat similar case was recorded in Öhringen, Württemberg in which, as in Ghent, the help the dowser was able to provide, was a 'subsidiary product' of whatever forces were at work.

The protagonist of the story was a Benedictine monk called Fidelis, a member of the community at the monastery of Neresheim. A picturesque character, a sturdy black-bearded friar of peasant origin, his reputation as a dowser and 'miracle-worker' was long-established. Again and again he was able to find wells and springs when geologists and other experts had given up all hope. In the neighbourhood of Neuenstein and Öhringen he discovered so many underground water-courses that the whole district was well-provided for a long time to come.

The geologists had stated some time before that the maximum yield would be a gallon or two per second. This verdict was apparently a hard blow for the town of Öhringen. Water was available—over an aquaduct that would carry it from the distant Ries area, near Ellwangen, but this was still being built, and it would cost a great deal of money—the little town's contribution would have been the equivalent of £100,000. Mayor Laidig and his experts were much disturbed by this prospect, as it would mean raising a loan from a bank at very high interest rates. Finally somebody suggested Brother Fidelis—who would cost nothing. After all, it was he who had discovered the large and plentiful springs in the Ries district which made the provision of water in Northern Württemberg possible over considerable distances.

Fidelis promptly answered the call of Öhringen and Neuenstein. And equally promptly, he found numerous underground streams and springs in the area of Neuenstein, which solved the drought problem.

It took three whole days during which the monk and the municipal architect, Herr Günzel, criss-crossed the whole district. Brother Fidelis obviously believed in making quite sure of success—for he had a pendulum in his right hand, a divining rod in the left. More than once, the pendulum reacted violently and the rod bent, pointing. The Benedictine monk counted the swings, moved to one side and then pointed the rod at a particular spot. 'This is the best place to drill,' he explained. And before the startled technicians could react, he provided them with the depth at which water would be found, with the rate of flow, the degree of hardness and a few other details. For the laymen all this sounded uncanny—and little short of witchcraft. 'But this is neither magic nor supernatural,' Brother Fidelis explained to his companions. 'All you need is thorough training, familiarity with the divining rod and above all, a definite sensibility for the radiation which the underground watercourses produce.' The Benedictine monk estimated the Öhringen water supply at something like more than fifty gallons per second —a very plentiful flow.

When the results were reported to Mayor Richard Laidig, he could barely speak. (The trial borings, made two days later, confirmed Brother Fidelis's forecasts in every detail.) Then he went to work with a will—preparing a new municipal budget. The city taxes could be reduced. To open up the underground water supply would only cost about £4,000 compared to the £100,000 that participation in the long-distance scheme would have meant, although the town decided to join the general scheme to help other smaller communities which needed the long-distance aquaduct. But even so they would save more than two-thirds of the original expense. They would be able to build a new high school, make a start on some council houses, improve street lighting—and all this because Brother Fidelis found water where no one else could.

A few weeks after these events when the underground wells were already linked into the town's water supply, the municipality gave a testimonial dinner to the Benedictine monk in the best restaurant. Everybody was there—including the whole personnel of the Town Hall, for Öhringen was a very democratic community.

It was a splendid social occasion which everybody enjoyed, including the caretaker and the two charladies who kept the Town Hall clean. But when next morning the Mayor arrived at his office, he found alarm and despondency. While he and his colleagues were celebrating Brother Fidelis's splendid work, burglars had entered the town treasurer's office, drilled a hole in the safe and removed the city tax receipts which were due to be deposited in the bank that very day. These amounted to about £80,000—and it seemed that Öhringen was right back in the financial crisis that had threatened to engulf it before the divining rod did its work.

The police were notified but did not get very far. Nothing like this had ever happened in the peaceful little town. Then the Mayor had a brainwave. If Brother Fidelis could find water many feet underground, surely it would not be impossible for him to find a gang of safe-breakers?

The Benedictine monk had never undertaken such a task and was somewhat reluctant to help, but in the end the desperate pleas of the town council moved him to agreement.

He came and spent some time in close proximity of the ravaged safe. His pendulum was again in his right hand, his divining rod in his left. It was the rod that started to point with a stubborn persistence—right down the corridor, down the staircase and into the caretaker's quarters. The police followed Brother Fidelis and Brother Fidelis followed his faithful twig of hazel. It led him into a small back room which the caretaker, distressed and confused, identified as his son's. But the boy was away, a student at Tübingen University. Surely he couldn't have had anything to do with such a wicked deed?

He could and he had. A couple of greedy girls, the drug scene and 'obliging' friends provided the motivation. The young student had heard of the planned celebrations and of course he knew the lay-out of the Öhringen Town Hall. Half-blackmailed, half-seduced into providing all this information, he guided the safe-breakers to their goal—and then was fobbed off with a very small share of the loot. Because Brother Fidelis, or rather his rod, had pointed the way, the criminals were arrested on the German–Belgian frontier. Most of the money was recovered. There was another dinner in honour of the Benedictine monk, but this time good care was taken that the municipal safe should not be left unattended!

Psychic diviners

We have already mentioned the involvement of clairvoyants in the Canadian kidnapping cases. Geof Gray-Cobb of

Montreal, an author, lecturer and psychic researcher, has an interesting additional story to tell about the incident which led to the brutal murder of a Quebec minister and the release of Mr Cross. Apparently, he was in the process of delivering a series of sixteen lectures on developing psychic powers when the story broke.

This is how Mr Gray-Cobb described the subsequent events: '. . . While the police were searching for the kidnapped diplomat, we reached the lecture on the pendulum. As an exercise, twelve students and myself used pendulums to dowse over a Montreal map to identify where he was being held captive. None of us found the right street. Three people zeroed in on St Hubert, across the river; two got nothing at all; six hit the north-east or eastern suburbs—an average of their "pendulum shots" centred on a spot some one mile east and half-a-mile south of where Cross was subsequently found. (This could be mentally biased, of course—the eastern part of Montreal is traditionally French, and the FLQ was certainly more likely to be hiding in the eastern part of the city, rather than in the more English west island.) One person got Dorval airport which is interesting because that is where the kidnappers eventually flew from. Yet no one hit the Cuban pavilion on the Expo islands from where Cross was released after negotiations.

'Lastly, the thirteenth member zeroed in precisely and accurately on 1635 Selkirk Street. That happened to be the apartment on top of the one we were operating in at the time, and it was inhabited by a mysterious band of hippies. I once again feel that some mental bias crept in there!

'Inconclusive as ever. I have read many claims of 100 per cent with pendulums, etc, but have yet to see it in action in twenty years of looking. In fact, I've got an involved personal theory that due to astrological and psychological influences, psychism works accurately only about 60 per cent of the time. When I see someone being 100 per cent successful . . . I start looking for the conjuring trick . . .'

This is certainly a singularly honest assessment of the achievement of dowser and diviner—though perhaps 60 per cent might be a rather high estimate of success. But even 10 or 20 per cent, if consistent enough, would be remarkable.

There is a French psychic who relies almost entirely on the pendulum for her results. Jeanne Couret, a charming Parisienne, has been described as '*un véritable phénomène électro-magnétique*'—whatever that may mean. While she has been tested by physicians and scientists, she has always refused to give public demonstrations of her talents. 'I would feel like facing the world totally naked. Even the presence of a most intelligent audience with hundreds of eyes fixed upon me would have a paralysing effect. And how often does it happen that psychics are thought to be either hysterical or deranged!'

But she has collaborated with a great many medical researchers who have been interested in the physical make-up of the 'sensitives'. Some told her that nine mediums out of ten suffer from thyroid troubles; among the women most have very fine skins and lack pubic hair. In a trance, Jeanne Couret's heart-beat slows down quite noticeably, and, according to Simone de Tervagne, who explored the lady's story and abilities, her 'electromagnetic qualities' are quite exceptional. Her father-in-law, a naval officer, told her never to touch a compass for if she did 'the needle went crazy'. She compared herself to a human electric battery: she had a magnetic potential which 'demanded to be discharged'. Thus when she did her psychic work, either as a diviner or as a clairvoyant, she was getting rid of her 'surplus magnetism', a necessity if she was to preserve her health. When she stopped, for instance during her brief and infrequent holidays, she felt ill at ease, 'congested, overcharged'.

'Some months ago,' she told Mademoiselle de Tervagne, 'I became luminous one night.' My husband woke up and told me that a greenish light clearly marked the outlines of my body. I felt very poorly, I was shaken by actual electrical discharges. Next day the newspapers spoke of an "electromagnetic phenomenon" which was observed the night before . . .'

She also has considerable difficulty in watching television. 'As long as I sit completely still, everything is fine. But the moment I get up to cross the room or bend down to pick up something, the images on the small screen become blurred or distorted. The set starts to crackle. I must sit down in my chair at a particular spot in order to ensure proper reception . . .'

Jeanne Couret reacted profoundly to atomic explosions—even underground ones. When the Russians conducted some underground tests in Siberia, she could hardly move for forty-eight hours. It was the same with earthquakes. Even if they took place thousands of miles away, she sensed them and could not sleep. 'I am a kind of radar screen,' she explained. 'I catch the rays, the emissions of people, the atmospheric vibrations, whether cosmic or subterranean . . .'

Born near La Rochelle, Jeanne Couret displayed unusual gifts when she was barely twelve; her family, alarmed by the manifestations of second sight, consulted several doctors. They were told that these were 'pre-puberty disturbances' and would end in due course. They did not and she was taken to a local healer, known as the '*Bon-Dieu de Saint-Just*', a somewhat daunting title. But Monsieur Monteau was quick to diagnose Jeanne's 'trouble' as a clear case of mediumship. He told her parents not to torture her with potions and cod liver oil, but rather allow her to develop her talents. They accepted the verdict—but insisted that it should be kept a secret.

She married very young; she studied singing but gave up a musical career after reading a book on the 'practical notions' of 'radiesthésie', written by a Franciscan missionary, Father Bourdoux, an expert in dowsing and divination. They became friends, and it was Father Bourdoux who presented her with her first pendulum—his own, treasured one. It was a simple stick of box-wood, pierced in the middle and suspended from a bit of twine. 'This is my most precious possession,' the missionary told her. 'I have never parted from it—all the time I lived in the colonies, in the jungle and in the great trackless grassy plains, I always carried it with me.'

Since then more than thirty years passed and Mademoiselle Couret has become one of the best-known and most frequently consulted sensitives of France. She has the most varied and most unexpected clients. Engineers and architects call on her for advice before they undertake major public works. Mostly they want information about the subsoil.

But she is also visited by writers and composers. Her pendulum, moving over a manuscript or a score, detects the 'weak points', the passages that should be corrected or rewritten.

Quite a few lawyers are among her clients whom she advises on the outcome of their cases. Art and antique dealers consult her about the authenticity of paintings and works of art. Her pendulum helps wholesalers to assess their markets. With the help of detailed maps she indicates underground springs, watercourses and the location of oil-wells. Again and again she has helped to find missing persons, and has aided the discovery of buried treasure—gauging the depth at which it is hidden and the chances of its recovery.

Simone de Tervagne asked her how she was able to operate in so many different fields, collect impressions from such varied sources.

'To tell the truth,' the diviner-clairvoyant replied, 'when I start I don't know which way I am going, what means I shall be using. I make myself submissive and "penetrable", I wait until my pendulum begins to extract the emanation from a photograph or a handwriting. The swinging of the pendulum enables me immediately to "see" the present, to sense the future. Sometimes I don't even need the rod or the pendulum. I only have to touch the object or the person, and I am off . . .'

She went on to explain that in principle when the pendulum swung to the right, it meant a positive response, while a left turn indicated a negative one. But it wasn't quite so simple, for everything depended on the 'polarity' of the person using the pendulum. If this was inverted, the normally negative must be considered positive—and vice versa.

'In our profession we are guided by quite precise laws. For instance, over the photograph of a dead person, the pendulum swings lengthwise. This is a mathematical rule. An experienced psychic does not even need a pendulum to find out whether someone is dead or alive. If he is dead, the photograph exudes a coldness. If he is alive, a certain amount of heat is released which one can feel very quickly. How can I explain this? I can't; it just happens.'

At the start of her career Father Bourdoux showed her the map of a large tract of land in Canada, not very far from Quebec. Jeanne Couret started to move the pendulum across the map. While her right hand held the pendulum, her left hand grasped a thimble which was filled with oil.

Before very long she was able to indicate exactly where, and at what depth, oil-deposits were situated. The Franciscan missionary took these indications to Canada where exploration and drilling began. Before very long oil was struck exactly at the place Jeanne Couret had foretold and the Laduboro Oil Company was founded. Monsieur Dubord, the director of the company, showed his gratitude by presenting Jeanne Couret with 2,000 shares in the company.

When the psychic senses running water, she feels as if her feet were immersed in it; similarly when she is seeking buried treasure, another curious sensation overcomes her—the feeling is of something drawing her into the ground by her feet, a sensation accompanied by a powerful tingling.

Jeanne Couret's work has regularly involved her in minor or major criminal investigations. When, in 1959, she was accused of 'practising medicine without proper qualifications' and faced a magistrate, three high-ranking police officials came forward as character witnesses and she was acquitted.

One of the people whom her counsel, the brilliant Maître Lévy-Oulmann, put on the witness stand was a Monsieur Jaquin, a baker of the Place d'Italie. He told the court that for many years he had consulted Jeanne Couret as to the quantity of cakes that he would need to prepare to satisfy his customers, and the pendulum indicated every time the correct figure—which was, of course, a great help to Monsieur Jaquin's business.

The lady also helped him to catch a thief who was systematically robbing him. She passed her pendulum over a ground plan of his shop and the adjoining living quarters and told him that it was one of his employees—someone he trusted implicitly—who was responsible. He was not only stealing money, but also pilfering large quantities of sugar, chocolate and biscuits.

The baker went to the police and they advised him to mark some banknotes and pieces of change with a little trace of paint; this he did and an inspector stationed himself at the back door of the large establishment. When the suspect left, he was stopped and searched. They found enough incriminating evidence on him as well as a large stock of stolen goods in his home—to send him to prison.

No wonder that Monsieur Jaquin was most eloquent in the praise of Jeanne Couret and even recommended her to a friend, an agent of a large flour milling company who regularly collected payments from the bakers of the *quartier*. One day he lost his satchel which contained a considerable amount. He had visited more than a dozen bakeries that particular morning and could not remember where he could have left the valuable bag. Madame Couret made him retrace his steps in his mind—without speaking a single word. When he reached one particular spot, she called out and said: 'That's it!' She told the excited bill-collector that the baker in question—whom she described as a man with an unusually long neck and a bird-like face—would at first deny any knowledge of the satchel but if he, the collector, insisted, he would return it.

Everything happened as Madame Couret foresaw it. When the collecting agent demanded his property, the baker at first pretended to know nothing about it, but his wife pretended to start looking for it and finally produced it from a drawer where she had 'put it by mistake'.

Once, in a single month, the medium was able to identify half-a-dozen criminals whose identity had been hidden from the police and who had committed a series of armed robberies.

Jeanne Couret has developed another method of using her pendulum. She suspends it over a photograph—preferably an unretouched, amateur one—and wherever it stops, she claims that she is able to discover patterns, designs, objects, details which for her represent tell-tale symbols. These she is able to interpret for her clients. She once found a royal crown in a photograph of the painter Alejo Vidal-Quadras and told his wife, the actress Tilda Thamar, that her husband was going to be commissioned to do the portraits of royalty—which, in due course, he did. She forecast to the novelist Juliette Benzoni that she was going to write a book about Napoleon which would also be filmed—finding the 'signposts' in a photograph of the authoress. She discovered a huge black cross (to her, the symbol of death) in a snapshot of the fishing boat *Poppy*, taken at La Rochelle—and within a couple of days the boat sank with the loss of all on board.

One day a lady came to see her and showed a photograph of her husband. Jeanne Couret's pendulum pointed to a strange image she detected in the branches of the tree under which he was standing. It was the menacing face of a witch-doctor—complete with a feather head-dress and a ferocious grin, a truly frightening visage. When she pointed this out to her visitor, the woman turned pale but remained silent.

'You've just returned from Africa with your husband,' the clairvoyant said. 'He is threatened by a witchdoctor who is determined to kill him. He is already under the shadow of death—or some grave injury.'

The lady explained that her husband had held an important position in the colonial customs service. He caught a native in a smuggling racket who, before he was taken into custody, snarled at the official: 'I shall pay you back for this! Take care!'

The very next week, on his way home, the unhappy woman's husband was involved in a curious accident; although a habitually cautious driver, his small car suddenly overturned for no apparent reason and his head was caught, as in a vice, in the wreck. It was several hours before he was released—totally paralysed. A series of extremely complex and delicate operations had relieved his condition somewhat, but the only hope that Jeanne Couret could hold out for the future was that he would regain the ability of speech and, in the course of some years, might be freed from the 'spell' which his enemy had cast upon him. Madame Couret showed Simone de Tervange a letter she received five years later that confirmed this prophecy. The clairvoyant herself has always had a firm belief in the reality of such 'spells'—regardless of whether the victim believes in them or not.

In this case, of course, she could not help. In another tragic case she tried her best—but was too late. She was visited by a young man, half-crippled, suffering from hereditary syphilis, a little simple-minded, extremely timid and hesitant. A bachelor, he lived with his mother whom he adored and who was his only support.

He spoke continually of his fear of losing her and remaining alone. Madame Couret tried to strengthen his self-confidence and free him from his black, morbid ideas. She asked him whether he had a photograph of himself. The young man took one from his wallet. When she looked at it and swung her pendulum over it, she noticed a strange superimposition that appeared to separate the head from the shoulders. 'He is going to lose his head,' she thought. 'Poor boy, he's going to lose his head.' But she interpreted this as a symbolic impression, not as tangible reality, although for a long time she could not free herself from the image.

Some months later she read his name and saw the same photograph in the newspapers. He had killed his mother and tried to commit suicide but failed. He was sentenced to death—and, as French law decreed, was guillotined. He literally lost his head.

Help from the ouija board

The ouija board is considered as a toy, or at the most as a highly questionable tool for communicating with the 'spirit world'. But, like pendulum and rod, it has been used in some instances as a highly unorthodox aid in criminal investigation.

A recent example was reported in the *National Enquirer* on 25 March 1973. Iain Calder quoted Chief Superintendent Pat Molloy of the Mid-Wales CID as saying: 'Eileen Gagnon and her ouija board managed to do what five months of intensive investigation failed to do . . .'

The case which twenty-two-year-old Eileen helped to solve began at the end of December 1972 when Michael Drinan, a forty-nine-year-old chef who worked in a Swansea nightclub reported the disappearance of his wife Laura. He seemed to be really distressed. On New Year's Eve he was seen in a local pub, weeping bitterly and complaining that his wife had left him. Later he even inserted an advertisement in a local paper appealing to her to return to him and their three children.

Eileen worked in the same night club—and she did not like Drinan. She found his behaviour a little too dramatic and his tears, to her at least, seemed crocodile tears. It was known that Mrs Drinan had a boy-friend (though she was fifty she was apparently still attractive and sexually adventurous) but the police had no clue as to what had happened to her.

The young girl kept her suspicions to herself—but went out and bought an ouija board. Then, in May 1972, she settled down to a long session with her cousin, Pearl Radlett.

The first question she asked was whether Mrs Drinan was alive. The marker, moving freely, pointed to 'no'. Then Eileen asked whether she had been murdered. The answer was 'yes'. Encouraged, Eileen asked the board for the name of the murderer. It obligingly spelled out D–R–I–N–A–N.

This jogged Eileen's memory. She remembered that a few days after Mrs Drinan's disappearance, her husband had brought a suitcase into the nightclub. So her fourth question was whether this had anything to do with the death. Again the answer was 'yes'.

No more information was forthcoming; but Eileen went to the police and told the chief superintendent what she had learned. Molloy was sceptical—but he thought that the information, however unusual its source, was worth following up. He went to the club and questioned several people working there. He succeeded in pinpointing the date on which Drinan had left the suitcase. It was 5 January 1972.

The suitcase was no longer on the premises and at first Drinan denied that there had ever been one. But finally, under persistent questioning, he broke down and told the police that he had found his wife dead in bed on 29 December. He presumed that she had committed suicide—and decided to dispose of her body. He put it into a trunk, took it to a deserted quarry, burned it with a flame gun normally used to burn weeds, and then dumped the remains into the sea.

The police went to the quarry, found burn marks and fragments of bone scattered around. A scarred finger with a wedding ring on it was also discovered. Enquiries showed that Drinan had rented a flame gun on 4 January, and when the suitcase containing Mrs Drinan's clothes was found at another club to which Drinan had taken it, a trace of human remains was established by laboratory methods.

Drinan's version of his wife's death was highly unlikely

and he was charged with her murder. A jury at Newport Crown Court found him guilty of manslaughter, deciding that he had killed his wife 'in a moment of passion'. He was given the comparatively mild sentence of six years. Chief Superintendent Molloy summed up his views: 'Without the help of Miss Gagnon and her ouija board, Drinan would probably have got away with it . . .'

Rose Stoler, a French clairvoyant, also uses the ouija board regularly. It was through this simple enough instrument that she helped the French police to track down a murderer—though only after he had claimed several victims.

A middle-aged lady came to consult Madame Stoler in Paris. It was in November 1968 and her visitor told her that she was under considerable stress, tortured by a vague yet constant anxiety. She travelled for a large firm of beauty products and lived in an isolated spot near Nogent-sur-Pise. Every day when she returned home by car after finishing work, she was seized by a mysterious, inexplicable fear. During the night she heard noises around her bungalow as if someone were trying to get in.

Madame Stoler consulted her ouija board—and the answers it provided communicated terror and menace. She 'saw' a man lurking in the shadows, hiding behind bushes, a man who held a weapon in his hand, ready to pounce . . .

'Your fears are justified,' she told Madame Thérèse A, her caller. 'The threat is gradually taking shape. I am convinced that for several days now a man has been watching you—and his intentions are evil. I see danger *coming from the shadows*. It is better if you arrange matters so that every evening one of your children accompanies you. This is important. And it would be just as well if you brought a good watch-dog . . .'

'That's not easy,' replied the lady. 'And as for being

accompanied—I can only arrange that for every other night . . .'

Madame Stoler suggested that Madame A should take a room in town for a few weeks. But apparently she couldn't afford it. Yet the more the clairvoyant concentrated on her board, the more definite the menace became. The man who represented the threat could be a lunatic, a dangerous psychopath. Rose Stoler felt deeply disturbed and also sad for she realised that however anxious Madame A was, she would not change her way of life.

Two days later Madame A was murdered by a man—outside her bungalow, at the moment when she was closing the door of her garage. The killer shot her at very close range, then crushed her head and dragged her body across the nearby railway tracks into some bushes.

During the investigation that followed, Madame Stoler's name was mentioned several times in the press reports, for after she had called on her, Madame A had told one of her neighbours about the clairvoyant's warning; she also wrote to her mother, saying: 'I consulted a medium, Madame Rose Stoler, whose ouija board warned me against the great peril which threatened me—against the danger *coming from the shadows* . . .'

The newspapers and the police asked Rose Stoler whether she could describe the murderer. On 29 January 1969, a description was published in the *France-Soir*. 'He must be about twenty-nine or thirty,' Rose Stoler said. 'Broad shoulders, stooping a little—brown hair. I don't think he is married—he hates women, in any case. His profession? Something manual. In his wallet I see a card with a tri-colour pattern. I don't know what it is. He's a Frenchman, he lives in the neighbourhood . . . very close to some woods; but he is not a neighbour of the late Madame A . . . He gets around on a bike or motorbike. Highly nervous. He has a little black book in which he enters painstakingly details about other women who live alone. *He is going to strike again . . .'*

During the following weeks several women narrowly escaped death in other, mysterious attacks. One of them, Madame F L, was struck by two rifle bullets and wounded when she arrived home in her car one evening.

Ten months later, in November 1969, the sinister 'shadow assassin' claimed new victims. He kidnapped Madame M and her daughter and forced them to walk to a deserted spot in the woods. Though she had been gagged and tied up, the young girl managed to escape and gave the alarm. By the time the police returned with her, they found Madame M dead—shot through the head.

In June 1970 a carpenter was arrested in a village 6 kilometres from Madame A's bungalow. A carbine was found in his home. His description fitted in every way the one given by Rose Stoler—except the colour of his hair which was black. However, it turned out that he had dyed it. He confessed to the murders and was found guilty but insane.

5
THERE SHALL BE NO TALK OF WITCHES

However far it appears from our subject at first glance, the strange psychological device known as the *Macbeth Prophecy* is completely pertinent to any examination of witchcraft and criminal investigation. For this special form of forecasting, the future has had a greater and more baneful influence on individual and collective evil than almost any other method of suggestion.

What are Macbeth prophecies? They are forecasts of the future which, deliberately or unconsciously, well-meant or malignant, *cause* to happen what they foretell. Fundamentally, they are not prophecies at all but either conscious or, more usually, unconscious suggestions. They insinuate themselves into the sphere of our willpower in the disguise of *precognition*—the most effective urge, for it excites our deepest desires. Their aim is to influence us, to smuggle foreign elements of volition into our own, to bend us to the service of an alien willpower. How dangerous and effective this is for the criminally inclined or the disoriented for whom the difference between good and evil is blurred, hardly needs to be emphasised.

The procedure of such a suggestion follows roughly this course: X finds it to his advantage that Y should carry out certain actions or change his will in a way that would be suited to X's purpose. But a direct transfer of volition (persuasion, pleading) meets strong resistance; even if it could be overcome, it would leave an uneasy feeling in Y. The obviousness of a direct transfer of will would mean that X would have to take responsibility for the suggested course of action—together with all its risks—for he would be the initiator. But, if X's words and opinions have sufficient weight and authority for Y, he can rid himself of such responsibility in advance; he can communicate his will to Y in the form of a prophecy. He can maintain that Y, having such-and-such a character, shall act in such-and-such a way. (If you wish to follow this in to the realm of religion, you may arrive at the doctrine of predestination, something that caused probably more misery than any other tenet, with the possible exception of the concept of the Chosen People and the present Pope's views on contraception.) Of course, X will depict Y's character in a fashion that suits himself, always keeping his, X's, own aims in view. Y, who is inclined to believe that X is a genuine judge of character and as such can form valid deductions, able to forecast the future, will now be under a double influence. Under the effect of X's description of his character, he will check and compare unconsciously all expressions of his personality with this 'character sketch'. He will keep those details in mind which are in harmony with the suggestion and forget the rest; he will soon reach the conviction that X's description of his, Y's, character is right. As this conviction develops, his belief in X's judgement is strengthened.

In this first phase of the Macbeth prophecy Y does not yet perform the specified action but he is already rushing blindly toward the second phase in which he is going to do it. Together with the discovery that X has hit off his character 'to perfection', he develops the view that such a perfect *descriptive* characterisation of human nature is *generally* possible; that human nature and character belong to the category of positive and exact knowledge and can be described and defined like anything else. If it can be described and defined while manifesting itself, it can also be calculated in advance, foretold in its activities and general direction.

In other words, human nature and character supply sufficient grounds for deducing future actions from present conditions. This is the classic clinical picture of the *fatalist psychosis*—the denial of reason, the fixed and lunatic idea that our actions must have a mechanical, causal connection with some definite psychological formula, the so-called 'human character'. (Or if you like, national, racial, class character.)

The unfortunate victim of this folly replaces his lost animate ego with this fixed and finite 'character'. After this he is little interested in anything but the events that are to happen. He becomes blind and deaf to the thousand possibilities of exercising his own will or fulfilling his own desires. Instead of a *subject*, he considers himself an *object*, replacing the first person with the third person singular. He feels that he has a 'task' to perform or—in the more serious cases—a 'mission' to fulfil and does not rest until he has made the content of the Macbeth prophecy fact and reality. Afterwards, there follows, in most cases, a complete split and collapse.

This would be the schematic description of the fulfilment of a Macbeth prophecy, a little simplified but basically true to life. In reality, of course, such a suggestion only represents a single factor among the many forces that shape our fate, our happiness, or our misery. But it has played and will always play a part as long as one human being is able to communicate his own thoughts and feelings in order to influence others. The thinking processes and the education and philosophical culture of modern man have made him especially susceptible to such suggestions; that is why the unusual dangers of these Macbeth prophecies must be emphasised.

Now and then, of course, it happens in real life that a Macbeth prophecy has a useful and fruitful effect. Usually this happens in cases when the 'prophet', due to some special disposition, is favourably inclined toward the person to whom he prophesies; he is likely to overestimate his subject and thus, unconsciously, it is the 'prophet' who is under the influence and power of the subject. (These cases, therefore, are not pure, but—one might say—pseudo-Macbeth prophecies.)

In the early stages of a love affair such prophecies can be especially effective; that is why a woman or man who is loved, grows beautiful, becomes worthier of and more suited for love—through love itself. This is the explanation of the 'miracles' that happen because someone believes in that particular miracle. Such a prophecy can be simply called 'a giving of confidence'. A good teacher knows its importance and employs it more or less consciously, like a hypnotist. A well-directed word of praise is a thousand times better encouragement for budding talent than a whole oration of criticism and carping; this is an easily understandable educational principle. But apart from education which, after all, is considered to be a science, any partisan (that is, unselfish) Macbeth prophecy can really work wonders in a favourable direction.

I have observed such miracles myself. One happened to a sensitive but otherwise insignificant artist. He had already reached the age at which the true genius produces masterpieces yet he was still turning out fifth-rate work bereft of any real promise. This happened in a small, central European country where a genuine hunger for culture existed side by side with enthusiasm engendered by the example of the great Western nations. Through a lucky accident this man was thrown into the middle of a restless, intellectual group. The small community not only hoped, but almost demanded with an unconscious prophetic fervour, the revival of the country's arts; eagerly, it sought a catalyst for its enthusiasm. Various crude signs drew their attention to the artist I mentioned. Suddenly, the myth began to spread that a great painter was born. A strange, paradoxical situation arose in which an artist acquired fame and general acclaim though nobody knew his works. Yet the explanation was very simple.

In those years the progressive elements were engaged in the feverish recruitment of a cultural army of which only a general staff existed. They were looking for a commander-in-chief. 'You don't know Z?' asked someone, surprised—someone who knew nothing of Z himself. 'Why, he is the greatest painter of our age!' And Z became a great painter before he himself knew of it; he rose to fame before his works had shown him worthy of such acclaim. And the miracle *did* happen; the famous artist began to paint much better pictures and in the end almost (if not entirely) achieved the heights to which he had been raised by such collective power, thus displaying the possible beneficial effects of a Macbeth prophecy in the development of hidden talent.

But generally the prophecy of 'it will happen because it must happen' is motivated by malignant instincts; its emphasis is provided by the threatening and ominous rumble rising from the depths of the subconscious. The prophecy expresses the desire of the prophet; and 'it will be' always means 'it must be', even if it promises a land of milk and honey—and even more so if it forecasts an apocalyptic disaster.

Vanity, excessive egotism, private interests, uncontrollable passions—these were the ingredients of the infernal brew bubbling in the kettle of the witches when Macbeth visited the blasted heath seeking to penetrate the veiled future.

The same ingredients were combined into the great historical prophecies of nineteenth-century materialism (world war, collapse, dictatorships) which were all fulfilled whereever the oppressed soul believed that it was born to live and die in slavery, and wherever the tyrant believed that he was carrying out a mission in practising inhuman cruelties and crimes. These 'prophets' told the bloodthirsty bandit that his robberies and murders were unavoidable; for the victim had already been prepared and persuaded not to resist, to resign himself to his fate.

We must remember that the power of spiritual resistance is in inverse ratio to the number of people involved; the mass soul is weaker, less stable, and therefore easier to influence than any of its individual components. Demagogues, charlatans and mountebanks are all well aware of this, and so are their clownish, drunken high priests, the political prophets, and it is the same in the story of every individual life.

Whoever recognises the danger of a Macbeth prophecy (and their number is decreasing), let him defend himself against it—and let him suppress within himself any inclination to such forecasts of the future.

It is easy to defend yourself, and though it may sound unlikely, it is easy to distinguish the true prophet from the false one. The false prophet wants no part of the Promised

Land, nor of any disaster; he never prophesies the future for himself, only for others. The true prophet, at most, invokes the prophecies of the old masters; he himself never raises the mirror of the future before you. He does not rattle Pandora's box in your ear but takes your hand—if you let him—and tries to guide you on the twisting, rocky road that divides again and again at each turning. It certainly needs greater courage to be an atheist than to be a pious believer in God and His heaven; it needs even greater strength to realise that the future is denied and curtained from all of us, including the most brilliant futurologist. We may believe that one turning leads to death, the other to life—but the true prophet will warn you at every turn that you can choose freely, that you have no predetermined path—the future lies within you.

Yet what has all this got to do with witchcraft, with black and white magic, and how is it relevant to detection and general police work?

King Coloman (or Kálmán) of Hungary, a scion of the Árpád Dynasty, reigned for thirty-four years in the late eleventh and early twelfth centuries. He was a bastard but of royal blood; he conquered Dalmatia and, to make his throne safe, used rather drastic methods against his own family—he had both his brother and his nephew blinded. But if his dynastic policies were harsh, he had some claim to be in advance of his age. He earned the sobriquet of 'Bookish', which indicated that he could read and write and had a weakness for the higher things in life. He is also remembered for a decree he issued in which he declared: 'There shall be no talk of witches who do not exist . . .' Historians still argue about the exact meaning of this royal phrase. Did Coloman intend to protect the innocent against unjust accusations without denying the existence of witches? Or was he enlightened enough to combat the witchhunting mania, a recurrent lunacy that endured well into the eighteenth century? *De strigae quae non sunt*, the Latin phrase ran. Certainly, the persecution of such persons ceased during his long span on the throne—even though it was renewed periodically in the subsequent century in even more civilised countries than his own.

The phrase, however, is a pertinent one. In Germany and in England, in Spain and even in colonial America, thousands of men and women died at the stake or suffered imprisonment and torture because of the belief in the existence of witches. Witchfinders Extraordinary like Matthew Hopkins (who, after three years of depredations, was caught in his own net and hanged as a warlock), the Scotsman Kincaid, the pitiless fanatic Benedict Carpzov (who was supposed to have sent 10,000 wretches to their death) flourished throughout the world. Peru executed the last witch in 1888; a woman was burned at the stake in Seville in 1781, and a girl beheaded in Madrid a year later. Quite a few of the victims confessed to 'extreme abominations' and some of them even gloried in the avowal of their non-existent powers and imaginary excesses.

These confessions, psychologically obvious examples of the self-destructive death-wish, were in reality Macbeth prophecies. For these could apply both to fiction and reality. The 'prophets' were the witchhunters, the sustainers and propagators of black magic. 'You are a witch,' they said, in effect, 'and you must conform to the marks and manifestations of witchcraft.' And a significant proportion of the accused not only accepted this but added to the fiction, embroidered and expanded the monstrous inventions. In tens of thousands of cases the Macbeth prophecy worked perfectly. In a way, it was a two-edged and easily reversed weapon—the more people were charged with witchcraft, the more admitted the charge which, in turn, strengthened the prosecutors and accusers until the mass hysteria threatened to engulf whole societies.

Today it is a generally accepted view that whenever a new religion supplants the old one, the latter is driven underground and becomes the hidden faith, the often garbled and transmuted creed. Much of it survives, heavily disguised, in the practices of the new, dominant church. Sometimes essential elements are borrowed deliberately or adapted for the conqueror's needs. (The fixing of the date of Christmas is a good example; the birth of Christ, according to the latest researches and theories, probably took place in August; but it suited the early Christian church to set its celebrations to coincide with the ancient Roman Saturnalia.)

With white and black magic, witchcraft, Wagga, or by whatever inexact appellation we wish to describe it, this process has been unique. The long underground existence of much of its dogma and practice has lasted almost 2,000 years. It surfaced time and again in the most unexpected places and the most exotic forms; but this was fragmentary, well-disguised and temporary.

However, less than a generation ago, a remarkable revolution took place. Witchcraft emerged into the open, covens became as numerous as Chambers of Commerce or Rotary Clubs; it seemed as if the old religion had gone over to the offensive.

There have been many complex reasons for this. The interest in the occult (of which witchcraft is both a basis and an important, constant element) has ebbed and flowed in the twentieth century; its peak was reached during and after the two world wars. But although the years 1916–24 and 1945–52 can be seen as 'boom' years, there has been no subsequent waning of interest. On the contrary, except in certain areas, the passionate concern with the occult has grown apace throughout the sixties and the signs are that there is going to be a sustained preoccupation with occultism —and in particular, with witchcraft.

One definite reason for this is the interest of *youth* in these phenomena. While in the twenties and thirties there were hardly any people under thirty among the members of psychical societies and research groups, or in the ranks of the spiritualist churches, the situation has changed throughout the world. In an *Esquire* article, Garry Wills has offered at least a partial explanation:

> A . . . sign of the empirical society is a reversion to superstition, magic, astrology, fortune-telling, I Ching, omens, spells ('Om'), Vedanta, witchcraft, mysticism. Not only do these supply a street theatre of liturgy, symbol and vestments; they are also, like all magic, basically experimental. Magic is a way of getting certain things done. When authority has been drained from conventional religion, when the social symbols no longer signify anything, no longer promote communication, men are forced to invent private myths; they are thrown back on pure faith, on undemonstrable mysteries . . . Magic is also 'against interpretation'. . .

Youth is primarily concerned in this process. The audiences that flocked to *Rosemary's Baby* or devoured the pseudo-Gothic romances about synthetic werewolves and imitation *revenants* were mostly the young. They also bought the ouija boards; and in drugs they sought the mystic experience, the 'total awareness'. This has brought an entirely new element and a vast new public into the occult field—as participants, as enquirers, as dupes and deceivers.

The other cause for this broadened and deepened interest in psychic matters, and especially in witchcraft, is not linked to any age group though perhaps it is again more evident in youth than in the more mature. It is the loss of belief in Reason in a world that has increasingly moved towards the *acte gratuite*. Pop art, the theatre of cruelty (and its various bastard offsprings), electronic music, unscripted and endless panel discussions on radio and TV, the *nouvelle vague* of films are just as much part of it as the murder of eight nurses in Chicago, the massacre of Sharon Tate and her companions in Hollywood or the Moscow gasman's rampage. The irrational has become a haven from the bankruptcy of logic and order. If the natural and reasonable are forsaken, the supernatural and the extra-rational must flourish. Our world no longer seeks normal logical explanations for the mysteries and rites of the occult; it is trying to substitute *mystique* for fact, the amateur's spontaneity for the professional's discipline—and, of course, is constantly seeking ways to commercialise all these aspects. If there are fewer mediums, telepaths or clairvoyants, there are more believers and seekers to consult them. Even scientists have been drawn into this magic circle, as they discover more and more surrealistic elements in their measurable and, until recently, classifiable and explorable world. What could be more surrealistic a conception than anti-matter and mirror-worlds, the entire heritage of Nils Bohr's complimentarity? Symmetry and system are being rapidly questioned; the alchemists have been proved at least partly right and old wives' tales about henbane and hellebore, spiders' webs and green mould have been transposed into digitalis therapy and antibiotics. And King Coloman's proclamation is both defied and confirmed. Today there is a good deal of talk about witches—who are called into existence by the talk. And here the three elements all meet—the Macbeth prophecy, the revival of witchcraft and the application of occultism to the endless and often heartbreakingly ineffectual and frustrated fight against crime.

Voodoo and Satanism

Society, as we have learned again and again, is not a static condition but a dynamic process. Few communities, if any, are immune to change—whether it be a monastery, Shangri-la, or a political party. This is a truism that is often forgotten or denied; but permanence and stability have become particularly ephemeral dreams in our century.

And if the societies change, if the flower children of yesterday become the political activists of today, and the pragmatic, 'working-within-the-Establishment' realists of tomorrow, there is also a great amount of interaction, mutual penetration and constant merging of even the most disparate elements. In Chesterton's brilliant *The Man Who Was Thursday* every member of the anarchist conspiracy turned out to be a police agent. In Tsarist Russia there were innumerable *agents provocateurs*, and there was at least one police chief who helped to plot the assassination of the mighty in the land. The double agent, the spy who serves two or three masters, is a hackneyed figure of the thriller today; yet who would deny his existence in view of the repeated defections, trials and revelations that fill the pages of newspapers? The young policewoman who, in May 1973, completed her assignment by posing as a drug-addict and securing the conviction of a whole group of London drug pedlars, is only one of the many 'double-agents' engaged in the pursuit of lawbreakers. Of course, apart from military espionage and criminal investigation, such a technique has been long extended into the political field—at least one American 'specialist' has confessed to infiltrating the campaign committee of Senator Muskie, and there have been literally hundreds who have served their masters in such a manner. This is not a defence or a condemnation of such methods; it is merely a statement of them. The Watergate affair, now threatening to engulf the chief executive of the United States, is only the most garish and most sensational example of the industrious beavers and termites gnawing at the foundations of the rival party, the competing business concern, the opposing ideology. The main rule seems to be: 'thou shalt not be found out'—and it is the most heinous crime if you are.

Why should the occult be exempt?

The land in which black magic still flourishes and is almost a state religion is the Republic of Haiti. Much has been written about voodoo that bears little resemblance to the actual thing. Certainly 'Papa Doc', late and unlamented, was said to have used it for his own purposes and his secret police employed several *Hungans* or priests. Actually, as Peter Haining records in his *The Anatomy of Witchcraft*, each Haitian ruler is supposed to fill simultaneously the post of the leader or Chief Hungan of the cult. This cult is a striking proof of the old religion surviving within the new one, of pagan elements merged into Christianity. For voodoo —or *vodoun* as its practitioners prefer to call it—was brought by West Indian slaves to the New World who thus salvaged their ancient gods and beliefs and created an enduring, if confused, amalgam of Christian and pagan practices.

I met a Haitian police official in California shortly after Papa Doc had died. He had to leave his native country because the young heir of the old dictator did not like him and he feared for his life—not only from the new president but also from the many enemies he had made during his long and by no means blameless career. He was a tall, plump man with a face of extreme innocence who made no bones about his past: he had killed and tortured, betrayed and persecuted scores of people in the service of his master. 'I wasn't born to be an underdog,' he said plaintively. 'And I always slept very well.'

It was logical that the plotters against Papa Doc should make use of the voodoo cult which was, in a way, the 'official' if underground religion of the Haitian Republic. At least half-a-dozen 'churches' were formed which outwardly conformed to the practices which the regime tolerated and even supported. In a country which suffered from one of the bloodiest and longest tyrannies of the New World, this was a kind of safety valve, an emotional and sexual release that could be controlled and directed. In a way it was similar to the methods of some European communist regimes who, at least in the early stages of taking power, encouraged pornography and eroticism. ('Give them plenty of flesh,' Matthias Rákosi, the sadistic dictator of Hungary was reported to have said during this critical period, although the word he used had four letters.) Thus the conspirators whose attempts to invade Haiti from Dominica and other bases had repeatedly failed, finally turned to voodoo. Any gathering aroused suspicion of the maniacally alert President; but the nocturnal celebrations of the ancient faith, with their attendant drunken sexual orgies, were tolerated. The anti-government underground exploited this tolerance and developed a secret communication system, woven out of voodoo and other elements, which enabled them to prepare for a general uprising in the tormented island.

It was foiled by the man whom I met in Monterey and who related his own part with relish but without any particular boasting.

'I had to play a triple part,' he explained, 'and it wasn't easy. It helped a little that my mother had been a *Mamaloi*, a voodoo priestess—though she had kept me out of her circle. She had ambitions, for me, you see—wanted me to get proper education, shake off the superstitions. She said that she was too far gone herself, she could not get rid of her childhood beliefs; but there was hope for me. She believed in what she was doing—but thought that she and her like were doomed, that in this century voodoo couldn't survive. So I had to start from the beginning. Luckily I remembered an old man everybody called Uncle Dave, a Jamaican-born ex-officer of the Haitian army. He had come down in the world considerably and was now earning a meagre living as a machine-cleaner in a cotton factory. At first he refused to believe that I knew nothing of voodoo—but I managed to convince him of my innocence. He was quite anxious to instruct me for he thought it a disgrace that I should be so ignorant. As a matter of fact, I encouraged him in the belief that I knew less than I did, though of course all my knowledge was second-hand . . .'

Uncle Dave spoke to him about the spirits that lived on the island; spirits no one could escape for they pursued white and black, rich and poor alike, until they possessed their body. Only the Papaloi and the holy priestesses, the Mamaloi, could control them and protect the individual from disaster.

'Worship the Green Snake,' the old man enjoined his pupil, 'for she is holy and in her dwells the soul of Damballa. Damballa the almighty on whose right hand sits Ezilée, his mistress. They are the great gods. Only they can defend you from the terrible blood-smeared demon, Ogoun Badagris. If you listen to the beat of the voodoo drums and worship with the Faithful, if you follow the gentle call, Papa Legba, the all-gracious will shelter you in his mercy. But when you hear the muffled poundings of the great Rada drums you will know that Ogoun Badagris must be appeased. Then you must go forth into the kingdom of Loco, god of the jungle, and at midnight you will receive with your brother sinners the baptism of blood. Only the blood sacrifice can cleanse your sinful bodies and prepare them for the dwelling-place of the all-wise Damballa. Voodoo is strong, stronger even than death . . .'

Through the old man, the secret agent gained entrance to the voodoo ceremonies, but this was the easier part; it was much more difficult to discover one of the resistance groups that used voodoo as a smoke-screen, as a convenient cover. It was several months before he succeeded and in the meantime, as he told me, a strange change had come over him. His Western education seemed to be stripped from him, together with his scepticism and sophistication. He reverted, at least to a certain extent, to the cult of which his mother had been a priestess. It was more and more difficult for him to preserve his detachment, to remember his assignment. He had almost 'gone native', regressed to the most primitive emotions. Then he met a girl through whom he gained entrance to one of the resistance groups. She was very young and had rebelled, when barely on the threshold of puberty, against the attitude of the voodoo cult to women; while the priestesses held considerable power, the rank-and-file female worshippers were treated as mere sex-objects, almost as if they were inanimate implements of the ritual. Her parents were wealthy but she had revolted against the comforts of the parental home and lived, with two other girls, in a shack on the outskirts of Port-au-Prince.

Their relationship began with her missionary zeal—to convert him to Trotskyism and to 'liberate' him from what she believed his submission to the voodoo ethic. Then he fell in love with her and she responded—because she found him a very willing and apt pupil. After they had become lovers, she introduced him into her revolutionary group. Its members were all young, naive and enthusiastic. His intoxication with the voodoo mystique had ended, and he played his part as a zealous convert to revolutionary action most convincingly. He was entrusted to act as liaison officer with similar groups and gradually learned the details of the whole network which wasn't large but did represent a potential threat to Papa Doc's oppressive regime.

His superior now became impatient and demanded results. He had not yet told him about his successful infiltration. But he could not postpone it very much longer. He decided to gather the final details—and then warn the girl that she was in danger. After all, she was only one of several dozen—if she escaped, the others still could be gathered into the net.

On the day when he was to meet her and tell her (though he had no intention of revealing himself as a government agent) he woke up shivering with a high fever. His condition worsened and by the evening he was delirious. His mother came to see him and as she ministered to him, she looked severe and grim. 'It is Damballa,' she told him in his brief intervals of lucidity. 'You have sinned against her. Now you have been surrendered to Ogoun Badagris. Perhaps I can save you—but I am not sure . . .'

He was too weak to protest that his was probably a minor infection, a touch of black fever. For many days he was terribly ill; the doctors could not diagnose the cause of his illness but his mother stayed at his bedside and after three long, exhausting weeks he recovered. Then he heard that the girl and her group had been arrested and were being held in an old fort, run by the secret police. He tried to get up to see her, or at least find out about her chances, but his mother, talking patiently and quietly as if to a five-year-old child, explained to him that it would be no use.

'She must be punished,' she said, 'and so must all the others. For she and her kind have sinned terribly against Damballa. They have mocked at her worship and tried to use

Ezilée and the others for their own paltry, selfish purposes . . .'

He tried to protest but as she went on, he began to realise that there was nothing he could do. The voodoo gods had struck him down because he had only pretended to believe in them; just as they (or the priests and priestesses) having once found out that the ancient worship was being used for a cover, had seen to it that the offenders were passed into the power of their enemies, the government and the secret police. For, in this respect, voodoo was impartial—it would deal with its opponents, punish the unbeliever, whatever his or her status, political philosophy or aim.

The girl and her companions were tortured and then sentenced to death. Papa Doc died two days before the date of their execution and so they survived. The man I met in Monterey had been only the indirect cause of their failure; he never met the girl again and soon afterwards he thought it wiser to leave the country. He was now himself a suspect —but, as he told me, he was far more afraid of what the Papaloi and Mamaloi could do to him. He had learned to believe in the power of voodoo even if he did not believe either the mythology or the ritual.

The Covens

Policemen and private investigators alike have repeatedly infiltrated into covens in three continents, from Vietnam to the Brazilian highlands, from England to the Far West of the United States.

When a friend of mine, one of the most outstanding criminal reporters, set out to penetrate the London and Home Counties 'black magic scene' he found precious little magic but a good deal of sex. Promiscuity dressed up in the trappings of occultism, the mumbo-jumbo of ill-digested satanism and devil-worship; group-sex and lesbianism, sado-masochism in its various graduations with occasional paedophilia and zoophilia. The grotesque yet haunting figure of Alistair Crowley still stalks the suburban streets and country vicarages, arm-in-arm with the shade of the Marquis de Sade.

Obviously, this development (sometimes secretive, sometimes well in the open) is of interest to the police—especially in our age when sex scandals and politics have produced unexpected bedfellows. There is at least one famous brothel in northwest London and another in central Paris where customers are titillated by a well-staged Witches' Sabbath, guaranteed to thrill—and help flagging potency. There is always a high priestess and if the 'virgin' required for the ritual would not bear clinical examination, she is usually a good enough actress to make her solemn, public deflowering quite convincing.

I have spoken to several policemen (and policewomen) in Britain, France and Germany who have joined covens to discover whether their practices went beyond the legal limits of play-acting and general foolishness. The answer was usually 'no'. Many of them had a mixture of cynical hedonists and 'true believers' in their membership; and though one or two—especially in Britain where this is a criminal offence—were prosecuted for keeping a 'disorderly house' or for pandering and procuring, these were cases in which greed got the better of discretion. The black magic part was the extra garnishing, the additional spice—though some covens were strangely strait-laced. Most of these were run by crackpots who, through their half-invented, half-traditional 'black magic', were fighting the established churches, and left the detritus of their nocturnal ceremonies in graveyards, deserted churches or at the crossroads. None of the police officers to whom I spoke found the slightest difficulty in joining the covens and being accepted as an earnest seeker for truth—but the vast majority also found that they were wasting their time.

Sometimes such an infiltration, however, could lead to tragedy. In May 1973 the newspapers reported the savage outbreak of a witchhunt in the Indian state of Bihar. Incredibly, rampaging mobs clubbed more than thirty people to death in a single week.

Scores of men and women, being suspected of practising witchcraft, were dragged off trains, out of shops and eating places and killed on the spot. Several old women were burned on bonfires. Characteristically, these had been prepared even before the victims were chosen so that they could be set ablaze before the police could arrive and rescue them.

It all began when rumours spread through Patna, the capital of Bihar, that witches were kidnapping children and adults in order to deprive them of their souls. No one knew how these rumours started, but before long they were being carried from the city into the countryside, even into the remotest areas. Within an amazingly short time they had covered the entire state like some black blight.

Both the capital and the larger cities of Bihar became paralysed by fear. Panic overcame even the better educated, intelligent minority. They had good reason to be afraid—because many of the victims came from their ranks. Someone only had to be accused of witchcraft for him to become an instant victim—it was like the Dark Ages of mass hysteria, a mere word being sufficient for a mob to form to mete out a painful death. Out of hundreds the police were only able to save half-a-dozen—more by accident than by planned action—for it was impossible to foretell which solitary old woman, gentle scholar or even child would be picked for a sacrifice to superstition.

As the killings continued, almost 150 people were arrested either for spreading the wild rumours or for participating in the lynchings. But this, of course, was only a fraction of the huge crowds on the rampage. Nor could anybody trace the whole hysterical outburst to its actual source.

Some of the unhappy men who were clubbed to death were members of Anand Marg, a religious sect. Apparently the only reason for their murder was that they had long sideboards left uncovered by their turbans and rather straggly beards. Others shared the same fate because they were cross-eyed, hunchbacked or had some other physical characteristic that set them apart.

The Bihar Government launched a vigorous campaign through loudspeaker vans, in cinemas, on posters and in newspapers, denouncing the rumour-mongers and appealing to commonsense, sanity and humanity. Unfortunately, as so many authorities have learned to their grief, public hysteria is one of the most difficult movements to stem. Some of the neighbouring states actually protested against the publicity given to the matter for they were afraid that it would spread to their territory.

It was much later that a clever reporter of the *Times of India* discovered the real origin of the witchhunt. Ironically, it was a police investigation that set it off. The federal police had been trying for a long time to find the principals of what they suspected to be one of the largest drug-smuggling gangs on the sub-continent. Because it was a large and widespread organisation, with links in political and business circles of impeccable respectability, they had to be particularly careful and discreet. At last they traced a substantial part of the gang to Patna. In order not to awaken suspicion of the others, several people were arrested and taken to police headquarters for questioning. The arrests all took place either late at night or early in the morning; and in all cases the entire family was taken into custody, including the women and children who were housed in the police compounds.

It was the disappearance of whole households—including the servants—which started the rumours. It was sufficient for one old servant (who had been absent on a visit when her employers and fellow-servants were taken away) to declare that some witches had spirited them away to set off the chain reaction. Inevitably, there were people who left their homes on various errands without telling their neighbours where they were going; some had gone on pilgrimages, others had unexpected business in distant places—it wasn't difficult to develop the theory of a widespread kidnapping plot by black magicians. The police could not disclose the truth for it would have ruined the investigation. As a matter of fact, as the trouble intensified, they were forced to release the great majority of the suspects—but by then it was much too late. Before it ended, the victims were counted in their hundreds. Thus, by a strange twist, the guardians of law and order became responsible for a terrible wave of lawlessness.

A somewhat similar story has been recorded in South Vietnam though without such dire consequences; in this case, however, the process was reversed.

A Saigon detective was assigned to infiltrate a sect somewhat similar to the Cao Dai, that unusual faith which combines elements of Buddhism, Christianity and Taoism, with a pantheon that includes Christ, Confucius and Victor Hugo. Only this particular church was based on a rather confused version of Manicheism, with additional contributions from the Paterniani, Venustiani and Lothardi—early deviations from Christianity. Like the Paterniani, they maintained that God and Satan each had an equal share in the creation of mankind, God being responsible for the upper and the Devil for the lower half of our bodies, so the 'satanic organs' of Man must be naturally used for 'the Devil's work'. The Lothardi, in the fourteenth century, declared that human beings should lead, generally speaking, a moral life—until they found themselves at least 6ft *underground*. *There* the rules of morality lapsed; the Vietnamese sect, like their distant predecessors, held their meetings underground. At least this was what one of their members (expelled for 'lack of discipline') told the Saigon police. He added that at these meetings the believers in this confused farrago performed 'horrible misdeeds of flagellation, sexual perversion, murder and suicide'. Also—which was what intrigued President Thieu's men most—they were plotting the wholesale assassination of the government, the top American advisers and the leaders of the rival religions in the country.

The religious and sexual aspects were of little interest to the Vietnamese police; but any political plot against an always shaky and only intermittently popular regime concerned them very much. So this young detective was detailed to worm his way into the secret and exclusive sect and discover the exact truth about their devil-worship and black magic activities.

After several months he managed to do so during the annual Tet celebrations. He had to make a substantial financial contribution to be admitted and the first two or three occasions he attended—all held underground, in the basements of burnt-out buildings or the cellars of abandoned temples and monasteries—amounted to little more than sexual free-for-alls, strictly heterosexual and quite enjoyable for the young investigator. It wasn't until a couple of months had passed that he discovered the real purpose of the innermost leadership of the sect, which had nothing to do with black magic, witchcraft or, for that matter, political assassination. It was simply a well-organised gang of thieves, specialising mostly in car-thefts from the American forces and government officials. Adjoining their underground 'temples' there were makeshift garages where the cars were repainted, number plates were changed, engine numbers filed off. The religious or witchcraft trappings simply served as camouflage to what was a highly profitable business. The gang leaders—the 'High Priests of Satan'—were arrested; but as the Saigon writer (who told me the story in Taipei) explained, quite probably the sect continued to flourish with other 'priests' and in other localities.

Witchcraft in California

As witchcraft (or its diluted and adulterated pseudo-version) emerged into the open and degenerated into a fad and a fashion, it also became more and more closely enmeshed with the so-called psychedelic drugs. A personification of occult sex, satanism and the magic of evil, Charles Manson and his 'family' slaughtered a number of people they had never met before—a perfect and gruesome example of the *acte gratuite*. As we know, though Manson and some members of his harem were sentenced to death, they escaped the California gas chamber because the Supreme Court of the United States had ruled capital punishment 'unnatural and cruel'. The trial itself was a six-ring circus —as most trials involving colourful and strong personalities are apt to be in the neophiliac United States. The multiple image which the proceedings disclosed was a fascinating one: Manson, the footloose wanderer, the frustrated magician, the hypnotic male whose women would do anything he asked them with the sort of utter masochistic submissiveness so alien to the mainstream of America;

Manson, the visionary and, finally, Manson the maniac whose supreme test for his followers was mass-murder—though he would not soil his own hands with blood. What he promised them, much in keeping with the practice of some far earlier black magicians, was a kind of black paradise on earth, totally within the experience of the senses. Most of these promises were redeemed through sex. His undisguised sadism was lightly wrapped up in much mystic talk, half-baked parable and lunatic precept. Drugs were added to sex as another means of achieving the 'mystic union with Evil that is the Supreme Good'. (How can you be redeemed if you haven't sinned? asked the early heretics.) Yet oddly enough at the same time Manson dreamt that his magic, which was embarrassingly amateurish, would bring him financial success, acclaim and material reward, and the Sharon Tate murders may very well have been due to the frustration of these ambitions. But it is evident that sex and drugs would not have been sufficient if he had not invented and elaborated an occult framework for them, namely the Manichean conception we have mentioned before, of Good and Evil being complementary, each being unable to exist without the other.

Craig Karpel, an American essayist, put it clearly enough in an *Esquire* article: 'The acid vision blends the illusory vector from good to evil into a circle.'

'M'Naghten's Rule, a courtroom test of sanity, does not enter it. Acid heads know very well the difference between right and wrong; it is the same as the difference between up and down, in and out, clockwise and counter-clockwise, a direction rather than a directive. That is why the leader of the Family that is up for offing Tate, Sebring, Folker, Frykowski and Parent could be called, interchangeably, God, Satan and Jesus by his zombies. There are few acid moralists. What is, is good; and what isn't, why, that's groovy too.'

Witchcraft had been linked to sex and drugs and so became even more fashionable—a trend and a fad within which evil is being celebrated 'with a flair for accoutrement and ceremony that will be merchandised to all of us in time'. *Women's Wear Daily* of New York published the classic report about this, when it wrote that the beauties of Manhattan were wearing diamond-encrusted crucifixes to ward off the Fiend. Or perhaps to attract him.

The dominating element in this half-mystic, half-hippy combination was, of course, LSD or 'acid'—the hallucinogenic drug that can be made at home from readily available chemicals after the briefest study of its preparation, and which has a fantastic potency in minute quantities. It inevitably links the psychic experiences of a 'trip' with sex—even though in most cases it is *sex-fantasy* rather than actual fornication, for acid, like most other drugs, is only a very temporary aphrodisiac and actually lowers the libido; or rather, turns it inward. As one 'tripper', a Los Angeles Bible salesman, explained in an interview: 'If you sense an evil here, you are right, and I'll tell you what it is; too many people turned on to acid. If you make a habit of tripping—well, acid is so spiritual, so metaphysical, that you are going to be forced into making a choice, between opting for good, staying on a goodness or Christian trip, and tripping with the Lord Satan. That's the whole heavy thing about too many people turned on to acid; to most of them, the devil just looks groovier. Acid is incredible—I've been on 172 trips now—but it shouldn't be available to everybody and anybody . . . Acid does expand the mind. I believe in powers that you can't explain . . .'

Confused, half-literate, conceited (for he, of course, is one of the elect to whom LSD should be available, who can control his reactions), these few sentences are highly revealing. They are the verbal and simplified equivalent of an action that a horrified friend of mine witnessed one day when a young man, under the influence of LSD, stepped on to a Hollywood freeway and tried to stop the traffic—because he firmly believed that he had the power to do so. Of course, he was reduced to a mangled heap of flesh within a minute or so. In the resulting pile-up three other people died and almost twenty were injured. Similarly a young girl, standing in the middle of a room in New York, on the twenty-seventh floor, suddenly exclaimed: 'I can fly! I can fly!' and before anybody could stop her, vaulted over the windowsill and plunged to death on the pavement below. 'Acidheads', LSD addicts, are getting increasingly involved in occult practices and cults—and many of them wear their large gold crosses to ward off the very evil which they worship and court.

In America some of these addicts are sons and daughters of wealthy parents who can indulge their various strange passions. I have seen them in California and in Florida, on Cape Cod and in Chicago, in New York and in Las Vegas; they are highly mobile. Their wealth has a high visibility even if its source is obscure.

One of the most striking and most outlandish characters in this constantly changing pageant is a woman who calls herself Princess Leda Amun Ra, neatly combining Greek and Egyptian mythology, merging in her person the daughter of Tyndaerus, King of Sparta, and whom Zeus impregnated in the guise of a swan—and the Sun God of the Nile. One of her hangouts was a huge, private nightclub on La Cienega Boulevard, within a short drive of the famous Sunset Strip of Los Angeles. It was called, fittingly enough, the Climax. There the privileged members sprawled on velveteen divans while ancient horror films featuring vampires were projected on the ceiling; or jerked and quivered in front of a 20ft high Satan's head, its eyes daubed with luminous paint. All this was more than a little reminiscent of the two adjoining, now defunct night-clubs of Montmartre (near the Place Pigalle) called *Ciel* and *Enfer* which combined witty obscenity with broad blasphemy. Here, sometimes, Princess Leda appeared—and she was a trifle more authentic than the phoney erotic setting. Her body covered with black feathers that appeared to sprout from her dead-white skin; her bare breasts (magnificently firm!) little restrained by gold fishnet. Her hair was ebony and her eyes huge and crazed. As she danced, she seemed to invoke the combined ghosts of Salome and Lility, Cleo de Merode and all the sex-symbols of the past centuries—and ours, too.

The Acid Goddess, as Tom Burke called her, had a male companion, a dashing young man who might be Mister Universe, dressed in red tights and top boots, his frilly shirt open to the waist, a sword in a scabbard on his lean hip. He was supposed to be an astrologer who charged $1,000 for a brief and perfunctory reading. He liked to be called the 'King' just as she was merely known as the 'Princess'. In a city where everybody was playing a part (in the hope that one day he or she might be called to do so in front of a camera) these two walked together wrapped in mystery, exuding an aura of decadent and yet powerful sexuality which was nourished by drugs and the occult. Leda played her part to the hilt, as Tom Burke's description made it only too clear when he presented the scene which he was allowed to witness in the Princess's 'castle' high above Hollywood: '. . . The boudoir, painted predominantly black, is large but the bed is almost too large for it—wide as two YWCA rooms side by side, canopied in black bombazine. In the bed, the Princess Leda Amun Ra, doe-naked, her skin dusted with pumice, or volcanic ash. She lies on her back, her legs splayed. Her thighs are firm as a girl's. Between her thighs is a full-grown black swan, its neck arched like a cobra's, its yellow eyes fixed, amazed. It makes one harsh, comic noise, like an echo from a rain forest.

"*I will conceive,*" the Princess shouts, heaving joyously. Half-a-dozen people have come into the room by now. No one else makes a sound. No one laughs; no one even smiles.'

There is no record whether the Princess ever produced an egg—or two—as her mythological ancestress did. Perhaps her turned-on associates could be made to believe even the miracle of half-human, half-avian miscegenation.

Behind this garishly outlandish scene—as a couple of FBI operatives who infiltrated the various satanic cults of California related—there were hidden far more material and sordid purposes. At one time even the Mafia was reported to be interested in the combined sex and drug scene. Later this was found to be untrue; for the various godfathers thought it incompatible with their Catholic faith to be linked with such heathen practices. Also, by and large, they found these operators small beer indeed—and, basically, rank amateurs. But it was through one of the psychedelic communes that in the spring of 1973 one large drug-smuggling gang was brought to justice. This operated between Mexico and northern California. The FBI agent who succeeded in being accepted by the practitioners of black magic actually rose to be the High Priest of the coven by dint of careful preparation and superb acting. In this capacity it was he who actually went to Mexico and brought in a large heroin shipment. This was removed by two of his colleagues from the airport locker where he had hidden it; but he was clever enough to persuade his group that the discovery was due to a police dog's well-trained nose. So he was able to divert two, much larger shipments of drugs before he shed his costume as leader of the group called *Inferno* whose members were arrested and received long prison sentences, while their counterparts in Yucatan were also rounded up.

If the drugs are mind-expanding, they are also apt to remove inhibitions and block the self-defence mechanism; some LSD addicts apparently feel an irresistible urge to tell all. It is particularly useful therefore for the police to have a 'plant' ready to collect this information, because even though it is often confused, heavily symbolic and contradictory, experts are able to evaluate it fairly easily.

Occultism and sex also merge in the various varieties of Satanism and witchcraft; as we have seen, these have not only lasted well into the sixties but seem to be developing and spreading. Much of it is just slightly ridiculous and childish pretence, self-conscious and deliberate 'naughtiness', but some of it is much more intense and much more dangerous. Like the Big Sur party I attended where the guests were received at the door with a welcoming drink—a bit of 'acid' and a pinch of strychnine mixed in tomato juice which at least had the colour of blood. They were supposed to empty the cup before they were admitted—for everybody had to be 'tripping'. The man who introduced me into the select company knew that all I wanted was to observe, not participate, and with his help I managed to skip this part of the proceedings.

Inside the house overlooking the Pacific three altars were set up; two of them had young, nude boys tied to them with wide leather belts, being whipped by two bearded men who were dressed in nuns' habits, looking more than a little incongruous but very determined. For whips they were using heavy black rosaries—and there was no make-believe about the flogging, for both boys were screaming and weeping. The middle altar held a girl, barely in her teens, with her arms and legs spreadeagled. A tall man wearing a goat's head was crushing a live frog on her sex, and he then started to carve a small cross on her bare stomach—just a shallow, superficial cut which, however, drew blood. Later the party became both wilder and more ritualistic; the young girl was deflowered in a long and elaborately blasphemous procedure, and then proceeded to retaliate on the goat-headed chief satanist with the help of a plastic dildo; this was followed by a kind of rock concert with songs whose lyrics were childishly yet persistently blasphemous, and it all ended with the declamation of a visionary creed by the 'Anti-Christ' which could only shock those who hadn't read the works of the late nineteenth-century decadents and Satanists.

The Anti-Christ is also a leading character in 'the Act of Evil' which neatly links sex and the occult. Its practitioners—some of them not without talent—believe that the Second Coming has already taken place, but instead of Jesus it is the False Messiah who has returned. (And this goes back to the legend of Zwi Sabatai, the Jewish False Messiah who was both a historical and legendary figure and played a decisive catalytic rôle in the diaspora's philosophical and religious development.) It is both amusing and characteristic that this reincarnated Satan is supposed to have chosen Hollywood Hills for his headquarters, whence he is supposed to have spread his tentacles throughout the world. He is served, so some of his believers claim, by an international organisation called the Devilmen who have admitted Satan into their bodies and souls and work for him. (This time a leaf is taken from the book propagating the totally fictional existence of the Elders of Zion, the anti-Bible of the Nazis and anti-Semites; a fabrication that has survived a dozen incontrovertible proofs of its complete phoniness.) This organisation or league is supposed to have become a secret world power whose members hold key positions in all major governments. But there is still hope for the forces of Virtue and Goodness; the Cross will triumph over vampires and devils!

The Devilmen have also been infiltrated by law-enforcing agents, but they found little criminal activity, except a little pot-smoking and some rather confused political and religious anarchism which was not illegal but merely ineffectual.

Of course, the close relationship of the drug-achieved psychic experience and sex has its elaborate and profitable—but quite legitimate—commercial side. Indeed, the three elements: hallucinogens, witchcraft (whether based on black or white magic) and sex in its most permissive, least inhibited forms, fuse into quite big business. Whether your special interest is reincarnation, numerology, the Cabala, astrology or Karmic law, it is all catered for by scores of shops and hundreds of merchandise items. Crucifixes are sold to the 'straight believers' and upside-down crosses to the Satanists. Zodiacal signs are bought by all and sundry; so are voodoo candles and love charms, amulets and incense. Today there are, according to a specialist, well over 1,000 bookshops in Western Europe and the United States that concentrate on occult literature, and in America alone their sales have tripled in recent years. The owner of the Magical Mystery Museum in Los Angeles who calls himself Arch-Druid Morloch, Bishop FAM (Family of the Ancient Mind—and why shouldn't he?), prides himself on his large collection of witchcraft items, and never lacks students at his 'college' which offers no less than thirty courses in the occult. He believes that 'the public wants to know more about the occult but will only be attracted by the spectacular'. Certainly, the goods on sale in some of the shops fulfil this requirement—from the carved devil's rosary, versions of the Egyptian ankh (symbol of life and fertility) to the all-seeing eyes, focusing spiritual aspirations; from satanic crosses, usually worn next to the skin, to Lucifer charms used in 'summoning the lower sexual spirits'. The Minotaur is a particularly popular 'love-sex-lust' charm and is often combined with a white disc, the 'replica of the seal of Solomon', representing the highest magical powers of the Cabala. And so it goes on, with prices ranging from a few pence to several hundred dollars. Add to it the various long-playing records devoted to the same subject such as the Rolling Stones' recent *Witchcraft* which proclaims on the sleeve that it is guaranteed to 'destroy minds and reap souls . . .' The same shop that will sell you an ouija board or an 'incantatory instrument' will also provide a mojo-bag love-charm consisting of 'love powder', pure mercury, 'Lucky John, the Conqueror', a root and 'love oil'. And it is true to say that whether in New York or London, Paris or Frankfurt, you are never too far from your 'friendly neighbourhood purveyor' of occultism and sex.

This proliferation of merchandising has occupied the police in many countries—mainly because so many of the shops (though by no means all of them) have been fronts for less esoteric and far more harmful activities. Two, at least, in the harbour district of Marseilles have been found to serve as stations on the modern underground railway of narcotic distribution. They were unmasked by three French detectives, who, in suitable hippy disguise, were hired as assistants (there was a large turnover in personnel at these shops, possibly because the real owners, middle-level members of the drug-peddling enterprise, did not want anybody to stay too long and snoop) and managed to obtain enough proof to close them down. But others are still operating, not only along the Mediterranean but in localities as varied as Stockholm and Tangier, Chicago and Rio. And two Mexican police officials who tried to emulate their more successful, or perhaps more cautious, French colleagues, were found brutally murdered in Acapulco.

It is very difficult to check the goods in such crowded, richly stocked shops and to discover whether the powder sold as incense isn't really dried 'grass' or whether the joss-sticks do not contain some material that produces something less innocent than fragrance. It is an endless fight, hampered by the insidious propaganda that equates drugs with alcohol and tobacco, claiming that in this modern age we all have the right to choose our particular path to hell and oblivion. But the struggle continues, with casualties on both sides; battles are won even if the war itself is still far from being ended.

6 THE PARAPSYCHOLOGY OF CRIME

In 1929 as a young crime reporter I covered the trial of the 'furies of Tiszazug', four Hungarian women who, between them, were responsible for killing twenty-seven people, though the prosecution was only able to prove eight of the murders. Tiszazug, 'the Nook of the River Tisza', became a sort of symbol in central Europe of abject poverty, greed, stupidity and suffering. In a desperately poor country where unemployment was endemic and the peasant had a hopeless desire for land, the *egyke*, the single child, had become the rule lest the acre or half-acre its parents had managed to scrape together should have to be divided or even lost. There were old people, too slow to die, who had to be helped out of this world so that their heirs need not wait for the pitiful inheritance. Gyula Háy, the Hungarian left-wing playwright, wrote a shattering play about these women, a devastating denunciation of the feudal, absentee landlords, the fat prelates, and the corrupt politicians who held the land in thrall, who owned—a few thousand of them—80 per cent of the fields and meadows. Novels and sociological studies had been published by the dozen, but here was the ugly reality, without literary embellishment, in all its crude formlessness. For me, a city boy, it was a traumatic experience which strengthened my resolve—selfish, if you like—to shake the dust of my native land from my shoes at the earliest possible moment.

The psychologist whom the defence had enlisted was an old family friend. He broke the rules when he took me with him to the prison of Szolnok and into the cells where the four women were kept: Mrs Lipka (indicted for five killings), Mrs Sebestyén, Mrs Köteles and Mrs Hulyban who were charged with one each.

They were peasant women, wearing black kerchiefs, their voices a pitiful whine, their bodies broken and crippled. I had seen such women before—by the age of fifty or sixty they were deformed and debilitated by hard work and many pregnancies. There was nothing to set these four poisoners apart. They were without backbone, almost indifferent to their fate, full of complaints—and all of them believed in God. Talking to them, a layman would not find a trace of any psychological deviation—and as a layman, I was quite ready to judge them completely sane—or at least *compos mentis* to the same extent as any of the old peasant women. But the psychiatrist had some curious experiences in the cells of the Szolnok jail with these four poisoners.

'Sign your name!' he told Mrs Lipka, handing her a piece of paper and a pencil. Her hand trembling, in a large, unformed hand, she put down—her maiden name.

'You, too!' the psychiatrist told the other three women. And they also produced exactly the same signature—obediently, unthinking, their maiden names.

My friend wasn't surprised. Evidently he had expected

them to act exactly this way. And when he asked them next to put down their married names, they began to tremble and shake, their whole bodies quivering as if he had asked them to perform some monstrous, outrageous deed; they stared with terrified eyes at the doctor and it took much cajoling and persuading until, with many a sigh and groan, they did as he asked. It needed only a touch of extra psychology—parapsychology, if you like—to guess the cause. Before they married, these women were happy. The troubles, miseries, and misfortunes which had brought them to these prison cells, had all begun on their wedding day, and now they loathed every thought, recoiled from every memory, that was linked to the beginning of their tragedy. Some of my analyst friends told me that it was the same thing with the paraplegic or the paralysed—if you asked them at what age they were condemned to the life of the cripple, they would name, almost without exception, the year *before* they were struck down. If you asked a fifty-year-old prisoner of the wheelchair whose illness began when he was twenty-six at what age he became a helpless invalid, he would answer: 'I was twenty-five.'

It was only natural that my friend should ask about the four poisoners' dreams. He was a believer in psychoanalysis and even went beyond it—Freud had only flirted with occultism, but this specialist believed that it had a legitimate part in his exploration of the subconscious. Again the answers were curious. Mrs Lipka and Mrs Hulyban had the same dream night after night—the same incubus pressed upon their chests and held them in a stranglehold. Both dreamt that they walked along the banks of the River Tisza, the second largest in Hungary, watching the water flowing past. The ground was soft underfoot and as they trudged on, staring at the landscape, the loose soil suddenly started to slip under their boots and collapsed. They sank into the constantly yielding soil, struggling, clawing, gasping for air, trying to escape the ghastly stranglehold, the mass of soft earth that was robbing them of their very breath—and this terrible sensation of suffocation filled all their nights. One of them had another dream: when she walked along the river, she carried a brick and she thought that she would use it to raise a house; but the earth collapsed under her and she and the brick were buried under it.

Women, all in separate cells, all having the same dream. The psychoanalyst-psychiatrist explained it thus: minds that have the same structure, that have had the same experience may easily find the same nocturnal outlets, the same escapes or traps in the occult. They carried a brick in their hands when they were clutching the poison with which they killed their relatives; they believed they could build a new house, rebuild their lives—but then the earth collapsed and buried everything, the whirlpool opened beneath them into which they were inescapably drawn. When they awoke, dawn seeped grey through the thick bars of their cells.

Perhaps the symbolism was too primitive, the transference too simple, but these were primitive and simple souls—the analyst did not have to delve deep, seek for elaborate sublimations and devious disguises.

I heard Mrs Lipka tell her life-story which again provided plenty of clues for the parapsychologist and the psychiatrist alike. She was orphaned at the age of four. She became like a torn-up weed carried away by the storm, drifting from one home to another. At ten she was already a 'working girl' and after that she toiled, incessantly and eternally. She slept in the stables, she spent her time with animals—the very centre of her life was the hen-coop, the pigsty, the cowstall. She had never longed for a man. But her instincts stirred when she watched lovers, for she felt that there was happiness in love and she had never been happy herself. She envied those who had found this happiness. She was a kind girl—full of gentle goodwill. She wouldn't even crush a bug when it crossed her path. When she sought a new master or mistress she stipulated that they should not expect her to kill poultry—she hated the idea of taking life. There was no joy in the life *she* led. She only had affection for 'the beasties'. She never slept with a man until she got married—and it was her husband she killed. 'I'm almost going mad if I think of it,' she kept on repeating, repenting her crime most assiduously, denouncing all the grief she caused, the horrors she set in train. If she was asked why she had killed those she did, she replied that it was her husband who persuaded her to kill her younger sister because she had 'tricked them out of their rightful inheritance'. As for the women whom she supplied with poison to kill their husbands—she was sorry for them because she could see how much they suffered from the wickedness of their menfolk. She herself had been reduced to a 'human wreck' but she still felt solidarity with her sisters whom life had likewise tormented and maltreated; so, without any recompense or for a very few pence, she supplied poison to the exploited, beaten, humiliated women to put an end to their misery.

Similar unusual features were discovered in the minds of the other female poisoners. Dr Alexander Feldmann, a close collaborator of Sigmund Freud, had spent many weeks with the women and was to be an official observer at their trial. He told me: 'With poisoning cases it is a general characteristic that the poisoners do not consider poison any ordinary substance but *the gift of some demonic power*. Livy recorded a case when 200 Roman matrons poisoned their husbands at the same time. In fifteenth-century Italy there was a regular price-list of poisons. Erich Wulffen, the German criminologist, discovered that it cost 500 gold ducats to have the Sultan poisoned; the King of Spain's death was cheaper, only 150 ducats and the Pope a mere 100. Those who engaged in the preparation and administering of poisons are filled with a primitive but overwhelming sense of power. And for centuries it has been a typically feminine crime—with very few male exceptions. In *Medea* there is the striking sentence: "Best is to use arms openly—but the female hand is best-versed in poisons." Shakespeare also spoke of the motivations for poisoning: lust for power, hate of the husband, disillusionment in marriage . . .'

Dr Feldmann mentioned two old, very famous poisoning cases whose parapsychology showed remarkable affinities with the Tiszazug women's crime.

'Margarete Zwanziger was born in 1760; just like Mrs Lipka, she was orphaned in early childhood. She was driven from pillar to post; at eleven, like Mrs Lipka, she became a servant. Then she married a notary who was many years her senior, and whom she did not love. He died and left her in the direst poverty. She came into the house of a law clerk where husband and wife lived in great discord. Margarete poisoned her mistress in the hope that as their housekeeper the widower would choose her for his second wife. But her hopes were disappointed. She moved again and became a young man's housekeeper. When he, too, proved reluctant to marry her she fed him poison as well. Next she took a job in the home of a married woman with a young child. She poisoned her new mistress, too, hoping that this time the husband would marry her. But she was still unlucky—and so she killed the half-orphaned baby. She was small, almost a dwarf, with ugly features that nobody had ever seen creased in a laugh. But her manner was ingratiating, servile and sycophantic. She was totally embittered by the world, believed everybody to be her enemy because no one had ever loved her. The contemporary legal experts declared that she had been driven by some irresistible force to commit the murders; she thought that poison could open up a new path, take her from the life that meant so much unhappiness . . .'

There was the other, even more famous poisoner—Madame Voisin, a classic case in forensic psychology and in parapsychology, too. She lived around 1670 in Paris when the French capital was teeming with poisoners and almost everybody was trafficking in potions, pills and powders. She was one of the most industrious and most successful. She had such a mysterious and all-pervading reputation that those who carried out the poisonings did not feel themselves guilty—they were completely under Madame Voisin's sway. Strangely enough, there was a similar character in the Tiszazug; the Hungarian Madame Voisin was the local midwife who handed out poison to all and sundry and in the end poisoned herself.

Dr Feldmann argued that in the case of forensic responsibility it was no longer possible to maintain the orthodox psychopathological attitude, considering only the physical, clinical elements. Parapsychology and modern abnormal psychology put a considerable emphasis on the *role of passions* in mental life; psychic and psychological abnormalities must be judged quite independently of physical fitness or illness. His theory approached the occult when he said that there was partial and general forensic irresponsibility, open and hidden motivations. There were those who confessed their crimes, fully explaining them—but the forensic psychologist saw clearly that these confessions and explanations were essentially untrue. The criminal acts were not motivated by the causes and urges expressed by the criminal but by important and hidden elements within his mind that fatally influenced his reason and his inhibitions. The poisoners of Tiszazug gave quite a straightforward explanation as to why they had committed their murders but these, too, were superficial and untenable. The motivations were partly occult, that is, inexplicable merely by psychopathology; they included the belief in the demonic power of poison, in the 'ghostly commands' they were supposed to obey. In addition, the setting in which they grew up and lived, together with the social, mental, cultural and economic poverty in which they vegetated, contributed to the final conclusion: the murderesses were sane and responsible in the ordinary, legal sense—and yet abnormal, irresponsible in their psychology and parapsychology.

The four women were tried and convicted, sentenced to life imprisonment. And, of course, there could be no other verdict in that period, in that particular country. Those who were really responsible for the terrible conditions that created the poisoners could not be called to account—yet in only twenty-odd years they and their whole class were to pay a traumatic price for their sins of omission and commission.

The Experts' Views

It is, of course, rare enough that the occult is accepted as a valid element in criminal psychology, or that the psychic elements are taken into serious consideration in police investigation—even though the understandable resistance seems to be weakening in some countries and in some respects. In recent years I have talked to a good many experts and while it is impossible to draw general conclusions, some of their views might provide a lead, a fragmentary yet discernible pattern.

One of the first I spoke to was Dr Ervin Hoepler, at one time Chief State Attorney of the Austrian Republic. Dr Hoepler was concerned with one of the most important and most frustrating human factors in forensic work—the problem of witnesses.

'Our main trouble has always been—and this seems to be universal,' Dr Hoepler told me, 'that most witnesses do not simply relate their own, personal experiences but also their views and deductions based on them—and present both as the actual truth. And you must add to this the innumerable and inevitable sensual delusions and deceptions. The general mental mood of the witness at the time of his observation also colours his testimony. Take three different people who were present at some incident: someone who walked along the street, deep in his thoughts; another, who stared through the window to distract himself; and finally a policeman on traffic duty. It is certain that the testimony of all three will be totally different.

'Memory, of course, also plays an important part and in this respect we are all widely different. The lacunae and slips of memory are particularly frequent among the injured. I have encountered cases when the lapses of memory were artificially induced—by hypnosis. In a provincial town two young men hypnotised a girl, and then had intercourse with her. When she came out of her trance, she was hypnotised once again and ordered *not* to remember anything that had happened to her. In this case, at least, they were successful. When she was questioned by the examining magistrate, all the girl could recall was having gone for a walk. It was the task of the police surgeon (himself an experienced hypnotist) to remove this memory block, and after a couple of sessions she was able to give a full and truthful account of the events. At the trial itself the whole process was repeated. The rapists would have been acquitted—for the law excluded the use of testimony under hypnosis—but they were so staggered by the failure of their stratagem that they confessed.

'I have found many paranormal elements in the behaviour of witnesses—that is, elements which were inexplicable by the present standards of psychology or, if you like, orthodox science. In police practice it is usual to take a witness to the scene of the crime—for the original setting is likely to aid the memory. A woman, for instance, only recognised the man who had assaulted her when she saw him on the same spot, in the same light. But I have also had cases when the mood or character of the setting itself influenced the testimony—one girl who had witnessed a murder told us that when she was taken back to the place the whole sequence of events was projected on to the empty clearing as if it had been a screen, and she was able to describe details which she *could not have seen* at the time the crime was committed. Was it implanted in her subconscious? Or was there, as some people claim, an "emanation" visible only to her?

'Such a support or strengthening of memory can bring results from the suspect or accused himself. It is, of course, general usage to take such a person to the scene of the crime for a reconstruction or questioning. And the "silent witnesses", the objects, the scenery, both have an automatic, undeniable influence on such occasions. Even if the suspect denies his guilt tenaciously, his resistance often weakens under such circumstances, his will becomes paralysed, and he is, quite often, prepared to confess. You might, indeed, speak of an occult influence of the non-organic world, an atmospheric, intangible effect that has been confirmed by innumerable experiences in my own career.

'There are similar elements in the personality of a witness—quite independent of his education, intelligence and reliability. Usually it is possible almost at the outset to establish from a gesture, an inflection or some other sign, what his attitude to the accused or suspect is. And sometimes this attitude is determined by psychological and psychic elements that cannot be measured by normal standards yet certainly exist. Of course, the testimony must be evaluated accordingly. There is also a considerable difference in this evaluation according to age and sex. There is, for instance, the problem of children. They are, on the whole, tremendously impressionable and malleable and keep on changing their statements. Perhaps the only value of such testimony is that, by and large, it is unmarked by love or hate, political or religious bias. Is there a particular sensitivity which links the young child to some earlier state of mind, a previous existence? Sometimes it seems there is—but the criminologist must not indulge such fancies. Young boys with open minds and sufficient courage are good observers. In their teens they already have certain guiding principles and are able to resist outside, alien influences.

'On the other hand the testimony of adolescent girls is usually unreliable. They are full of romanticism, crushes, enthusiasms—and vanity. They like to exaggerate, especially if they find themselves the centre of attention. A simple theft becomes robbery, rudeness is turned into rape, a light-hearted conversation is classified as an attempt at seduction. Quite a few innocent people have gone to jail because such testimony has been accepted in a tense atmosphere or through inflamed prejudice. On the other hand there are certain cases in which teenage girls are excellent witnesses. If the case involves a young man living in an opposite flat, an interesting, pretty woman or a young couple, their observations are acute and accurate. The best witnesses, we have found, are adult, mature men. By and large men will emphasise the intellectual, reasonable motives and elements while women will favour the emotional ones. With elderly people one must always take into consideration their past experiences, the triumphs and failures that they had lived through. Some of the older witnesses are lenient, inclined to peaceful solutions—others are bitter and ruthless. The very old are comparable to the children. And there is, of course, the questioner, the prosecutor himself—he must guard scrupulously against his own moods influencing him, he must exercise the strictest self-control in order to preserve his objectivity. I must say that among my colleagues I have found those who had faith in survival after death, in the supernatural—whether in a religious or in a simply ethical form—the most effective. This might surprise people whose approach to criminology and the forensic sciences is purely materialistic (as, indeed, to a large extent it has to be)—nevertheless, at least in my experience, it is entirely true.'

Dr Paul Gartner, another psychoanalyst who has also worked for several years as an official police and court psychiatrist, spent a good deal of time examining the psychology of ex-prisoners. Among other things, he talked to me about the ideal technique of questioning people under arrest.

This should respect the complete psychological and physical freedom of the suspect; the questions should only be aimed at making the subject communicate fully in the most relevant direction. A stenographer should record literally all the slips, the hesitations, gaps, unfinished or repeated and modified sentences which a person is apt to produce if suspicion about him or her is justified. The record should also contain the suspect's lapses of memory, contradictions, fantasies, dreams and psychic revelations; all this, of course, in addition to the pertinent factual statements. At a later stage the suspect should be placed in a reclining, comfortable position, with eyes closed. A simple apparatus controlling breathing and pulse is then attached to his body which, while it allows complete freedom of movement, projects the recorded heartbeat and breathing on to a screen or a sheet of opaque glass behind him. (Dr Gartner himself developed such an instrument some years before the lie-detector was perfected.) The questions would be posed on the basis of free association, a well-tested psychological method. If the suspect resists communicating some idea or image that occurs to him spontaneously, repressing or modifying it, this entails an emotional, mental effort, an inhibiting process. And this in turn is reflected in the nervous system, in changes of the pulse-rate and breathing—because the passions and emotions linked to the repressed truth find a physical outlet. The proper system of questioning establishes clearly the areas of such self-repression and discloses the causes of the inhibitions. Certainly, an innocent man's anxiety or the emotional associations of a frank confession in the case of a guilty person both follow this process. But the differences between them form distinct categories and typical graphs, and with some experience, it is easy to recognise and identify them.

It was in the early 1930s that Dr Gartner developed these methods though he did not have sufficient opportunity to put them into practice. But already he was advocating the use of certain 'mind-liberating' drugs. In cases of crimes involving material gain the subcutaneous injection of a combination of mescaline and caffeine and a spoonful of strammonium could 'disconnect conscious critical faculties'.

For periods varying from thirty to sixty minutes the subject established a rapport with the questioner that deprived him of the ability of speaking an untruth—even when it served his own most obvious interests. The possibility of error and misleading intent was so slight that it could have no practical influence upon the efficacy of the investigation—and if it did, subsequent control could easily eliminate it. Dr Gartner made it clear that this method must be applied humanely and justly—that is, apart from the police doctor or medical expert, the suspect's lawyer must also be present.

When I talked to him, Gartner was optimistic. 'The successive instances of criminal justice,' he said, 'recognise more and more clearly what is fundamentally and eternally human: the possibility of error and the fictitiousness of judicial certainty. That is why, with the methods I suggested, one can help the activity of the police and achieve more and more reliable results in ascertaining the facts . . .'

He added: 'Parapsychology is still a very new science and many people deny its right to be called a science at all. Yet there is a twilight zone between them—and we are not yet properly equipped to explore it. But that doesn't mean that we can afford to deny its existence.'

Gartner also gave much thought to the idea and practice of *a criminal record*. He considered both completely irrational, for anybody could learn of a person's previous convictions which meant that, having served his sentence, he could not regain his place in society unhindered. Such a record was not only a grave handicap for an ex-convict because the certificates and references needed to create a new existence or perform some official act invariably compromised him, but also because someone with such a record inevitably moved with less certainty, with more inhibitions among those who were without one. This was one of the explanations why such an individual tended to associate with others who also had such a 'past'. Shame and modesty were present in the psychology of a former jailbird, and only among his equals did he not feel the disgrace of being a marked man. 'There are certain propositions for reform,' Dr Gartner explained, 'which would extinguish the criminal record after a certain period of time had passed. But these are also mistaken because the fate of a released prisoner is usually determined by the first few months; it is exactly during that period that he has to find a place, become a useful member of society. And in this he is just as much handicapped by the present usage as by the wrongly conceived reform suggestions.'

'It would be rational to declare,' the expert continued, 'that after serving his sentence a criminal becomes in every way the equal of his fellow-men. Only the criminal authorities should keep track of his record, and no one else should have a chance to find out about it. At the most it should be considered a subsidiary penalty to be applied for anti-social behaviour in the prison or an immediate relapse after release—but only for a definite period of time. It is psychologically rational to expect that someone who has "paid his debt to society" should wish to return to the community as an equal, guaranteed the same chances and same opportunities as the others.'

Was this being too soft on the habitual criminal? I asked. 'No,' Dr Gartner said, 'for he would be excluded from such tolerant treatment. And while there may be certain abuses, these would be more than balanced by the social and economic benefits.'

He had also done much research into the hygiene and alimentation of prisons. The facilities for accommodation, diet, access to fresh air, etc., still, he felt, needed global and urgent reform—it should not be a matter of indifference to society whether the discharged prisoner had contracted some serious stomach ailment or tuberculosis.

'Even if such a person is cured,' Dr Gartner explained, 'the fact that he had contracted the ailment while in prison may have the most serious psychological consequences. The grudge that all criminals bear society—however disguised, sublimated or suppressed—is naturally strengthened by such a physical handicap acquired during imprisonment. It is both good economic sense and an act of social responsibility to prevent this. Then there is the superficially trivial problem of smoking—which, however, has a tremendous importance for the prisoner. It is incredible how many problems this has created and continues to create; the greater part of prisoners concentrate with desperate eagerness on the single perquisite of freedom—the right to smoke. But most prison systems forbid it strictly. Psychologically, smoking is an oral-genital pleasure that sublimates many passions. It should be obvious that the tension inevitably created in the emotional and libidinal world of the prisoners should be lessened, and if smoking can do this, it should be permitted within reasonable limits. It would be a safety valve that would probably save lives and prevent endless trouble. Nor should some kind of entertainment or pastime be neglected. Most prison libraries are grossly inadequate; there is a lack of educational works which are also entertaining. How much could be done for the individual progress of the prisoner (and the interest of the community) if he were given a chance to fill the gaps in his education, acquire new skills and develop existing ones. All this could be easily done with a properly individualised and truly expert library-policy, with language and vocational courses. Theatrical and film performances of suitable, selected plays and pictures could also contribute to this important task . . .'

On the Continent the jailed criminal found scant sympathy except from the visiting priests and nuns. None of these had any authority to change or influence the prisoner's lot; while they might be the best-informed, the most familiar with the problems of each individual, practically they could do very little for them. 'Every member of the penitentiary organisation,' Dr Gartner explained, 'should be imbued with the spirit of guidance and re-education. Affection, trust, sympathy can only be created by persons possessing the same qualities. Adults cannot be educated by simpler means than children. There has been no comprehensive study yet about rational pedagogic methods in prisons, nothing to provide clear directives. Yet the disadvantages of the actual practice in these institutions are felt by the taxpayer and by society in general, at least to the same extent as parents, unversed in the right principles of education, feel the evil wrought, the trouble caused by the unsuitable, bigoted teachers . . . We have to create forensic psychologists who possess what I would call, for want of a better word, a sixth sense—a compound of understanding, humaneness, telepathy and clairvoyance. And if this is asking too much, think of the price we are paying for our failure to find and train such people!'

The Twilight State

Another forensic psychologist with whom I discussed the same problems was Dr Ernst Bischoff, a professor at Vienna University. He pointed out that the psychology of crime had occupied more and more writers and scientists in recent years. Alienists were particularly interested in these extremely grave problems. In the thirties there was an increasing number of outstanding experts who took the view that crime was basically a psychological (and even parapsychological) phenomenon. Lombroso (much misunderstood) had proclaimed this theory first but modern psychology and its new methods have opened much wider perspectives for the researches of criminal psychologists. These researches have established that there was a strange, almost occult transitional stage between rationality and madness. German specialists named it *Dämmerzustand*, twilight state. It was about this that I asked Dr Bischoff's opinion.

'To begin with,' he told me, 'one must make it quite

clear: until now no such twilight, "misty" condition could be observed in completely healthy, normal people—or rather those whom we call by such names under a rather loose terminology. But what is this state, this condition? Nothing but the intrusion of another ego, the subconscious personality into the realm of the conscious ego; the partial slide or fall of the conscious ego into a visionary world. In order that this should happen in some individual, a pathological pre-condition must exist. In many people this strange disposition to this twilight, transitional condition is quite evident, easy to observe—with others it remains hidden for a long time, until some external event intervenes and its sudden effect triggers off the slipping or sliding into the *Dämmerzustand*. In such a condition a person might commit actions which, once the twilight period is over, fills him with the greatest horror, despair and regret. Of course, such a condition has a thousand different manifestations and there are many transitory stages between the actual twilight, befogged state, and other disturbances and fluctuations of consciousness. Most of the people who are obedient slaves of their visionary twilight condition are recruited from the ranks of epileptics, hysterics and other physically or mentally handicapped people. With epileptics it often happens that after an attack there is a temporary disturbance of the consciousness. During this time practically all contact between the person affected and the outside world becomes interrupted.'

I asked him about the basic characteristics of this *Dämmerzustand*, which—to me at least—suggested the trance condition of mediums or the hypnotic sleep of responsive subjects.

'There are several varieties of it,' replied Dr Bischoff. 'In some cases the patient is unconscious, incapable of thought or action. In other cases, however, he enters the subconscious, occult world actively, positively and lives this second life with still greater intensity than the first, conscious, real one. With epileptics the most dangerous circumstance is that this twilight condition often arises in them even without an attack—lasting sometimes only for a few seconds but often for hours, even days. On the whole epileptics are always irritable and hostile to their environment. Therefore frequently the slightest incident is sufficient to create extreme excitement and lapse into such a twilight state. To provoke this, some visionary experience is quite sufficient, resulting in the same excitement as some external impression. Quite often this ends in some criminal action—though of course, this does not apply to all epileptics, nor to epileptics alone. Sometimes the destructive rage of such people is directed against themselves and the results are terrible self-mutilations or suicides. Many inexplicable suicides are due to such occult influences which parapsychology has barely started to explore . . . I had recently a most interesting case. The patient was a prisoner who tried to hang himself with his twisted bed-sheet. Luckily he was cut down in time. The most curious circumstance was the subsequent total amnesia —he could not remember at all what he had done or what motives had brought him to the self-destructive act. We went into his medical history and discovered that he had suffered from epilepsy; he had made several previous attempts to kill himself but he did not recall a single one. Whenever he slipped into such a twilight state, his hate and rage always turned against himself.'

The psyche of these people was full of mnemonic gaps, Dr Bischoff explained. Certain sections and points of their lives are completely wiped from their brains. 'It is as if some non-physical and extra-sensory power had passed a sponge over certain areas of their minds.' Unfortunately this symptom does not much help the forensic psychologist, for many criminals simulating madness use it as a clever trick. Therefore other factors and symptoms are necessary to establish whether the criminal he is asked to examine really suffers from such mental lapses, blocks and hiatuses. The best indication seems to be the fact that after committing a crime and emerging from the twilight condition, the subject falls into a long, deep sleep of exhaustion. Many of them behave with apparent, total normality in their *Dämmerzustand,* able to deceive even their closest relatives and friends. Others fall into convulsions, their faces become distorted, they stammer, stagger or become totally insensible to physical pain—showing a close parallel with hysterics and saints.

Sometimes there is a complete split of personality in the twilight condition. Dr Bischoff quoted the classic case of an Englishman who, in such a state, boarded a ship in a British port and sailed for India. The journey took weeks and he remained in his twilight state without anybody noticing anything unusual in his behaviour. He emerged from it when he reached Bombay and was dismayed to find himself on another continent. He could not conceive how this could have happened to him.

The cases of the hysterical twilight state are also extremely interesting. In such a condition those afflicted strive for dramatic effects, strike theatrical poses. Often they commit various trickeries and impostures under a practically unconscious constraint. It is in such cases that the parapsychologist and forensic expert finds it most difficult to draw the line between the true *Dämmerzustand* and play-acting or simulation.

'Once a young lady visited me,' Dr Bischoff said, 'she bore the name of one of our oldest and most distinguished aristocratic families. She was accompanied by her solicitor, one of the best-known attorneys of Vienna. In the first few minutes she made the best possible impression—young, elegant, intelligent. Then she related a complicated, most romantic love affair. She told me how she was seduced, locked up in a nunnery and had to escape in the most adventurous manner. She recounted all this with such convincing realism that she could have rivalled the very finest actress. In the end it turned out that the elegant, refined lady was a hysterical servant girl, guilty of a whole series of crimes, whom her counsel had brought to me for examination. She adjusted herself so brilliantly to her visionary condition that she could have misled the most acute experts . . .'

The borderline between psychology and parapsychology is very often just as vague as the *Dämmerzustand*. No wonder that orthodox alienists shun this misty terrain as if it were plague-ridden. And in more modern times the confusion has mounted, the role of drugs and cults has infinitely complicated matters. It is more convenient to adopt a purely materialistic, behaviourist attitude—until the sceptic is forced to invent the most fantastic supporting theories for his doubts. For few, indeed, have the humility to say simply: 'I do not know.'

Others, like Karl Jentsch, try the historical approach.

It was he who told me the story of a Bey of Tunis who died in the 1870s. He was reputed to sit in judgement once a week, administering justice in his own august person. The delinquents were paraded, their misdeeds briefly described and His Highness passed sentence immediately—by using one of three gestures. Either he passed his hand horizontally in front of his throat or he swung it through the air or he rubbed his thumb and forefinger together. The rope, the whip, the fine. And as he was by no means a cruel man but a highly pragmatic one, he chose, whenever circumstances permitted, the third alternative. Idealists might find this illimitably simple justice highly objectionable, but while no reliable data existed about morality and public safety in Tunisia at the time, one could claim *a priori* that the Bey of Tunis, with his basic procedure, proved to be a true father of his people. He got at least as far as we in the West did with our complicated jurisprudence, forensic wisdom, legal shrewdness, court eloquence, public debates and general brooding—all to make the punishment fit the crime, or to decide whether any punishment was to be administered at all.

Jentsch pointed to the morass of nonsense, baseness, cruelty and misery through which Europe had to wade until it arrived at the present, highly unsatisfactory state of affairs. The beginnings, he said, were not so bad. The barbarians of the North were neither softhearted nor sentimental, a foot or arm hacked off was no great matter—but they were free of *aimless* cruelty. In the early Middle Ages, Jentsch explained, corporal punishment was rare; there were no qualified death sentences. The criminals were punished either by having to do religious penance or pay compensation. In the half-secular, half-religious Carolingian empire there was a mixed system. For a long time royal judgement followed the same procedure: the local feudal lord (the *Sendgraf*) and the bishop toured the parishes of their fief and bishopric every year; the community gathered in the church where there stood a table with a crucifix, some rods and a pair of scissors beside it; the parish priest or the village elder presented the cause of the sinner; if he was found guilty, he was promptly scourged (that is, if he was a serf) while a free man had his locks shorn—for long hair was the symbol of freedom as it seems to have become once again with today's youth—after which he was locked in a monastery for a while. Of course, in those times the monastery was an all-purpose institution—acting as a school, a training place for all public servants, an agricultural college and experimental farm, an academy of art, a library and . . . a prison.

Obviously, with all these functions, the monastery brought a supernatural, religious and occult element into the various disciplines and activities. Above all, this coloured its attitude to crime and punishment, to demonic possession (which could account for so much) and to the irrational elements in human behaviour. All this, as long as church and state administered justice jointly or at least in reasonable harmony, had a decisive influence on medieval criminology and parapsychology.

But between the fifth and tenth centuries the poor Europeans had to endure the constant incursions of cruel foes: Huns, Avars, Magyars, Normans, Saracens. People were massacred or dragged into slavery in their thousands and young boys, for instance, were forced into sodomy and became the inmates of homosexual harems of pashas and beys. It was natural that revenge and retribution should follow. First came the bloody subjugation of the adjoining, non-Christian countries. Then ensued almost endless feuds and petty wars. In Italy practically every city and town became an armed camp, divided into warring factions. Thus, gradually or abruptly, people became used to the shedding of blood, compassion was dulled, understanding clouded. Finally Roman jurists and ecclesiastical inquisitors arrived and brought, with their abominable court proceedings, method into the madness of cruelty. This madness was so evil that compared to it, Charles V's draconic laws appeared to be quite mild. As trade and industry began to flourish at the end of the Middle Ages, both the chances of gain and the intensity of greed increased—and so did the number and severity of penalties for crimes against property. In England from 1400 onwards these penalties became steadily more extreme, as Westermarck showed. As late as 1837 a nine-year-old child was sentenced to death because it had broken a shopwindow and stole tuppence worth of paint.

Dr Samuel Ettinger and others have examined the history of criminal procedure and penalty and shown that the barbaric periods have lasted far too long. They have also presented the thinkers and philanthropists who, by the eighteenth century, managed to achieve certain long-overdue reforms and mitigations. Yet even in more recent times the anthropological school of criminal theory has caused a good deal of harm. The old theory declared that criminal law had only one purpose: to repair the breach of law and order, considering the reform of the criminal and the protection of the society as mere subsidiary aims. The newer, more recent tendency, which has had a considerable influence on penological reform, has proclaimed these two goals as the main task; it seeks to establish the causes and motives of crime and to remove them, to cure the disease rather than deal with the mere symptoms. We have seen in recent decades that, in spite of constant setbacks, hygiene, social policies and crime prevention have become the main concern of those who believe in the possibility of rehabilitation and reform. Certainly, Lombroso's theories, however eloquently presented, have been totally disproved by now. There are no 'born criminals' or criminal types. Today we know that the criminal cannot be recognised by some outside, physical characteristics—even if such characteristics might have a bearing on his treatment by society and thus on the conditioning life administers. No respectable and serious thinker believes today that criminality is atavism, a throw-back to primitive prehistoric man—for whom, if we followed Lombroso, crime was second or even first nature. Social anthropology has proved that, by and large, the so-called savages are far less anti-social than their more civilised fellow-beings. The work of Margaret Mead and her colleagues has amply proved this; even though there are few communities left which remain untouched by the dire effects of encountering 'civilisation'. And of course, there have always been many criminals who show no trace of the Lombroso characteristics such as excessive hirsuteness but lack of facial hair, small stature, protruding ears, a mis-shapen skull, etc. One could cite geniuses and the most respectable pillars of society who show such alleged 'marks of Cain'.

In the early years of the nineteenth century Dr Foissac presented a human skull to the French Anthropological Association. Many of the learned members examined it and came to the conclusion that the skull belonged to an inferior being, entirely dominated by animal instincts—and that he must have probably ended on the scaffold. They were rather dismayed to be told that the skull was that of Professor Bichat, the founder of general anatomy and histology, a pioneer of physiological medicine. Younger criminals, it must be an obvious truism, if decently dressed, could hardly be told apart from the law-abiding citizens. Only the prolonged practice of crime stamps them with a professional character—as, indeed, does every other profession. Long years in prison give them a look that sets them apart from the unblemished majority.

Socrates confessed that his nature made him capable of any crime and Carlyle thought that one should never explore the worthiness of a petitioner because every man (but not every woman) deserved the gallows—and therefore the granting of his request as well. All men want to be happy and if anybody hinders this striving, they automatically turn against those whom they see as obstacles. This might happen, according to the circumstances, in honest competition, in legitimate rivalry—but also in the form of crime. The decisive factors are mostly social. The man in the average, medium condition of life is least inclined to satisfy natural urges illegally, has the fewest incitements to do evil—something the ancients recognised. Carlyle, to support his views, cited Horace who praised the *aurea mediocritas*, the Golden Mean, and also the anonymous author of *Proverbs* who prayed: 'Give me neither poverty nor riches.' But the constraints and privations of distress naturally have a stronger effect than the temptations to excess or perversion in pleasure; and the poor, neglected and ill-educated in childhood, lacking in later years the help of family and friends, also lack the inhibitions which are implanted in the rich by virtue of their higher training, firmer character and the need for them to maintain their position of respect. Finally, the poor are less well equipped for conducting the struggle for life. (How much these premises have changed in the welfare state and with the growing levelling of classes, hardly needs to be stressed; but Carlyle's views were somewhat reactionary even for his age.)

Lombroso sacrificed his whole life to developing and defending a theory which, at first hailed and celebrated, was soon after his death in 1909 recognised as totally wrong. But the immense work which he had done was not entirely in vain—as the physiology and parapsychology of criminals have proved. His efforts led to the organisation of the study of forensic physiology. Because, taken globally, the vast majority of the criminals come from the lower classes, the proletariat, this has led to a close examination of their physical characteristics. Criminal attitudes are just as little inherited as infectious diseases are—but there is heredity in the disposition to both. Flabby muscles, shattered nerves, lowered vitality create much higher sensitivity to contamination and infection, there being less resistance to injury, less ability to repair and heal. Similar physical conditions create the psychological framework for criminality either because they make the sufferer incapable of regular and protracted work or because, as Karl Jentsch argues, they arouse pathological and dangerous urges. These inherited dispositions are rooted, of course, in social conditions for these have created the weak, misshapen or ailing bodies which parents bequeath to their children. So criminal anthropology is neither worthless nor wrong in itself—only in its exaggerated claims and in the misinterpretation caused by separating it from criminal sociology.

What of the parapsychological aspects of the problem? Obviously physiological and physical conditions influence mental attitudes; superstition and prejudice flourish in such circumstances. But at the same time it is a strange fact that most important mediums of the nineteenth and twentieth centuries have come from the working and lower-middle classes. Does this mean that privations sharpen the extrasensory perceptions? That the bridge-builders between normal and paranormal, natural and supernatural are more likely to be the deprived and underprivileged? These are questions that await examination just as the whole field of parapsychology must be widened, to include the wide-ranging tests of individuals rather than of phenomena. Here various disciplines must meet—and criminology is one of them, nor is it the least important.

The Future of Forensic Occultism

In October 1925 Sir Arthur Conan Doyle gave a long interview to a French journalist in which he forecast that the detectives of the future would be clairvoyants; or if they had no such occult powers, they would employ mediums in all their investigations. Police work would become infinitely simple—

any murder could be solved within the shortest possible time by psychometry. By handling some passion or piece of clothing of the victim, the medium would be able to describe in detail how and by whom the murder was committed.

Sir Arthur was on the eve of leaving for South Africa to give a series of lectures on spiritualism. He prophesied that spiritualism would transform the world: science, medicine, philosophy and the tracking down of criminals—but also the courts and the codes of law. And of course, religion would also be influenced by its progress. Humanity would approach closer to the mysteries of the unknown. He was convinced that in earlier times men were able to communicate with the heavenly spirits—but this link had been broken. Now spiritualism would renew the close connection of heaven and earth.

The creator of Sherlock Holmes was a somewhat indifferent prophet. Parapsychology, as Janet Watts explained in a *Guardian* article, published in June 1973, is still a 'fringe science'. There is no provision in the budgets of most police departments for sensitives and psychics.

Miss Watts was reporting on the London visit of Dr Helmut Schmidt, described as 'one of the world's most respectable parapsychologists'. Schmidt came to his present discipline from physics. He had been working both in academic and commercial research and became interested in extra-sensory perception through the work of Dr S. V. Soal and Professor Joseph Rhine. Rhine suggested to him that he should try a few tests on his own children. Schmidt was rather reluctant to do so, but in the end he went home and tried some simple tests (predicting the colours of chips) on his small daughter—who astonished him by scoring higher than the normal, statistical accuracy. Dr Schmidt had a very broad-minded employer, the Boeing Company, who gave him ample time for his experiments which had little or nothing to do with aerodynamics. Before very long he gave up his 'serious' profession and became director of the Institute of Parapsychology in North Carolina.

He has developed methods which exclude fraud rigorously and eliminate human fallibility. (Would it not be wonderful if these could be applied to police work?) His subjects are tested for powers of precognition and psychokinesis. And he has found that one in three people—quite ordinary, average citizens—shows above average powers in these tests. He has also found that 'psychic phenomena are very subtly related to mood'. Subjects need a lot of encouragement and tangible incentives, such as money, are also quite useful.

In America the scientific community has swung to the acceptance of parapsychology in the last forty years, especially between 1932 and 1952. In Britain a questionnaire which Dr Schmidt designed has revealed a vast and enthusiastic response among the normally sceptical and hard-headed readers of the *New Scientist*. There is, of course, still a very strong resistance to parapsychology. Because, as Mencken said, 'there is no sneer as cruel as the sneer of Academe' it may take a very long time indeed before Chairs exploring the unseen and the intangible are established at the major universities. There will be always the fear of deception, the taint of charlatanism.

Strangely enough, there are signs that in the forensic field this acceptance is likely to be far more general and accelerated. How much of it will remain unofficial—except, perhaps, in the United States—remains to be seen. The practical value of such help has been amply demonstrated; it is not a question of advocating this or that approach but to emphasise their practicability.

In this brief survey I have tried to indicate the various ways in which crime and the occult, criminology and the paranormal are intertwined. General conclusions are impossible and the actual cases, the details, are often contradictory and confusing. But as one high-ranking police official told me in the summer of 1973 in Germany: 'If someone came to me and proved with reasonable certainty that by using witch-doctors or astrologers I could reduce the crime problem in my city, I would be willing to accept the suggestion at once. For beyond any doubt we are losing the fight against the depredations of the modern criminal, the hijacker, the kidnapper, the extortionist, the psychopath—and we cannot be choosey about any help, from whatever quarter it comes.'

By no means all high-ranking police officials would share this view. But there is certainly a growing proportion of forensic experts who do.

SELECT BIBLIOGRAPHY

Chesterton, G. K. *The Wisdom of Father Brown* (1909)
——. *The Innocence of Father Brown* (1911)
Doyle, Sir Arthur Conan. *The Adventures of Sherlock Holmes* (1891)
——. *The Memoirs of Sherlock Holmes* (1894)
Frank, Gerald. *The Boston Strangler* (New York, 1964)
Haining, Peter. *The Anatomy of Witchcraft* (1972)
Háy, Gyula. *Tiszazug* (play, Budapest, 1952)
Hayek, Max. *Das Geheimnis der Schrift* (Vienna, 1922)
——. *Der Schriftdeuter Raphael Schermann* (Vienna, 1923)
Langen, Prof D. *Kompendium der medizinischen Hypnose* (Munich, 1972)
Mayer, Dr L. *Das Verbrechen in Hypnose und seine Aufklärungsmethoden* (Munich, 1937)
Poe, Edgar Allan. *The Purloined Letter* (New York, 1875)
Rohrschach, Dr Herman. *Psychodiagnostik* (Berne, 1923)
Rolfi, Pio Michele. *Magia Moderna* (Milan, 1933)
Royer, M. *Traité des influences et des vertus occultes des êtres terrestres* (Rouen, 1677)

Steiger, Brad. *The Psychic Feats of Olof Jonsson* (Boston, 1968)
Stockvis, Prof. *Hypnose in der ärztlichen Praxis* (Basle, 1955)
Stockvis, Prof, and Pflanz, M. *Suggestion in ihrer relativen Betrifflichkeit, medizinisch und sozial-psychologisch betrachtet* (Stuttgart, 1961)
Tabori, Cornelius (with Paul Tabori). *My Occult Diary* (1950)
Tabori, Paul. *Private Gallery* (1945)
——. *The Book of the Hand* (Philadelphia, 1961)
——. *Pioneers of the Unseen* (1972)
Tervagne, Simone de. *Les Exploratrices de L'Invisible* (Paris, 1970)
Tromp, Prof S. W. *Psychical Physics* (The Hague, 1963)
Vallemont, de. *La physique occulte* (Paris, 1693)
Völgyesi, Dr Ferenc. *Animal and Human Hypnotism* (Budapest, 1931)
Wagner-Jauregg, Julius von. *Suggestion, Hypnotism and Telepathy* (Vienna, 1919)

INDEX